QUILTING
NEW DIMENSIONS

ANNE COLEMAN

B.T. Batsford Ltd, London

First published 1989

ISBN 0 7134 5710 4 (cased)

Typeset by Lasertext Ltd, Stretford, Manchester
and printed in Great Britain by
The Bath Press, Bath
for the publishers
B. T. Batsford Ltd
4 Fitzhardinge Street
London W1H 0AH

Acknowledgement

I would like to thank all the people who allowed me to use photographs of their embroideries and quilting to illustrate this book. Thanks are also due to Alan J. Oates for help with photography and to Margaret Rivers for practical help and advice.
I would like to thank Christine and David Liddle for allowing me to borrow and to draw their family quilt. The picture on page 42 is reproduced by kind permission of Frances and Mike Nugent. The pebble (Colour Plate 15) is reproduced by kind permission of Iris White. The Octopus Garden is reproduced by kind permission of Anne and Colin Beales. Finally, I would like to thank Peter Coleman for his continuing support and encouragement.

Contents

Part Two: Using other materials to raise a surface

Part Three: Materials, tools and techniques

Introduction

Some methods used by craftsmen in the making of clothes and furnishings have been employed in a practical way for centuries and are still common today. Quilting is one of them.

Upholsterers use quilting, sewing together layers of cloth and stuffings which are then supported with wood and wire to make a three-dimensional piece of furniture. Corsetry involves the use of wire and strips of plastic enclosed in cloth to make a flexible material which is strong enough to hold in superfluous flesh. Tailors use stiffened materials like canvas and muslin to hold collars and cuffs in shape and milliners use stiffened fabric shapes to support tulles and chiffons. Cardboards and plastics are used to hold soft furnishings in position.

Textiles are used and manipulated in a practical way in the theatre, in industry and in the home. Many people are able to earn their living practising some of these skills and, with more leisure time, many people – both men and women – are able to pursue an interest in work with fabrics. A growing number of people have taken up some textile technique as an important leisure pastime and adult education classes in upholstery and soft furnishings are particularly popular. The stripped chair, lovingly upholstered, the boned wedding dress over stiffened petticoats fit for a princess, and the carefully constructed scenery for the model railway, all involve textiles which have been used as a means of self-expression as much as of function.

Many craftspeople, embroiderers and artists go one step further and explore and experiment with these same techniques and methods, using them to create pictures, wall hangings and three-dimensional fabric sculptures, with textiles as the medium rather than paints or stone or wood. Textiles are versatile.

Some purists feel that to experiment with traditional techniques is wrong, but as we look with great admiration at the construction of an antique costume or the flowing patterns of a handsewn quilt, it would be interesting to speculate on how, if they lived today, the people who made them might choose to employ their skills.

One of the exciting aspects of contemporary embroidery is working in depth where the work is raised from the background and can be seen 'in the round'. Fabric and thread are well suited to working in relief and in three dimensions as they are pliable

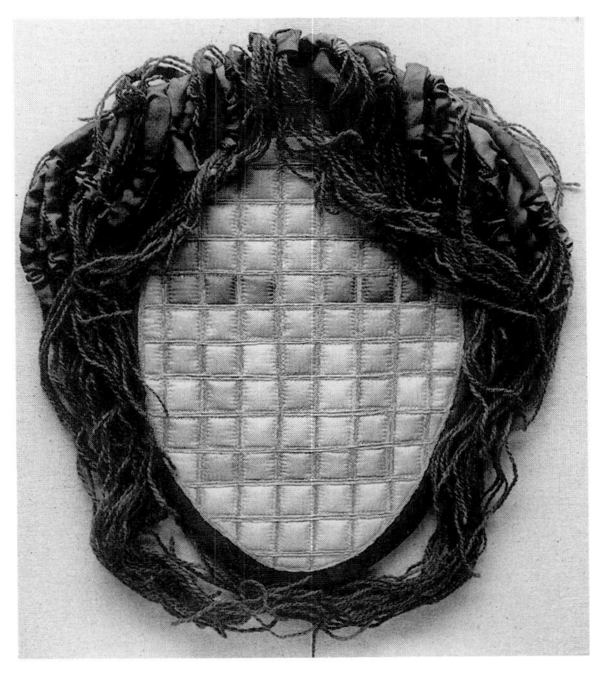

1 Quilted Head by Elizabeth Woodthorpe. Machine patchwork and quilting on hand dyed silk with rouleaux and wool 'hair'.

materials and will bend and fold and can easily be manipulated into different shapes.

Quite a number of stitches can be detached from the surface and made to stretch both from one level to another and also across spaces. Because fabrics are usually soft and floppy, however, they need to be held in place by some other medium. The supports can be traditional materials like wadding, stuffing, wire and glue, or newer plastic materials like foam and polystyrene. Sometimes the support is hidden, or it might show as an integral part of the design.

This book describes some methods of creating depth and raising the surface of embroidery, and of designing and making simple three-dimensional shapes, using the techniques of quilting, padding and stiffening. The importance of experimenting with the medium and the technique is emphasized, because this is the way of discovering new possibilities with traditional methods. There are also suggestions for trying out some of the techniques to create various artefacts and wall hangings.

Anything constructed on more than one level calls for extremely careful planning, so it is a good idea to keep a sketchbook or notebook to note the stages of construction if these are at all complicated. Each step should be worked out first, making a paper and sticky-tape mock-up if necessary, then the work can be carried out in the correct sequence.

Part One

QUILTING

1

Basic techniques

Quilting is an old and well-loved technique. It can be used either in a strictly functional or in a purely decorative way, or in a combination of both, so it appeals to a wide cross-section of embroiderers. It is such an easy technique that it is quickly mastered and the lovely raised surfaces that are produced are very pleasing.

The basic principle of quilting is to sew together two or more layers of fabric, usually with a thick layer of padding material between, either all over or intermittently. Quilting is seen in everyday garments like anoraks, and in furnishings like duvets and eiderdowns. It is commonly used in upholstery and soft furnishings for holding materials in place and creating a comfortable padded surface.

Quilting has been used throughout history as protection against cold because the layer of wadding caught between the layers of fabric acts as good insulation. People wore padded clothes and slept under quilted textiles for warmth. Quilting was common throughout the world in countries which had low temperatures for part of the year.

Strong fabrics like canvas were quilted and actually used as armour, and quilted garments were habitually worn under armour as protection against chafing metal. Quilting in its widest sense is still used today for protective clothing ranging from sports equipment to the bulletproof vest.

Commercial quilting is now done by machine and the modern practitioners of hand quilting are people who produce individual artefacts and enjoy quilting as an art form. The technique is particularly satisfying to many people because it gives plenty of scope for self-expression while producing something functional.

Although the types of fabrics and materials and how they are sewn together have given rise to named subdivisions of the technique, the fundamental idea is the same. However, the subdivisions are convenient to use as starting points, and they are as follows.

Wadded quilting, or English quilting (all-over quilting) Two layers of fabric sandwich a layer of stuffing or wadding, and are held together by a pattern of stitches. Wadded quilting is usually used for warmth.

Corded quilting, or Italian quilting (intermittent quilting in lines) This technique produces a pattern of raised lines on the surface of the fabric. Two layers of fabric are stitched together with parallel lines of stitches to form channels; these are then threaded with cords of thick wool or quilting wool. Corded quilting is used as decoration, either alone or in conjunction with wadded quilting,

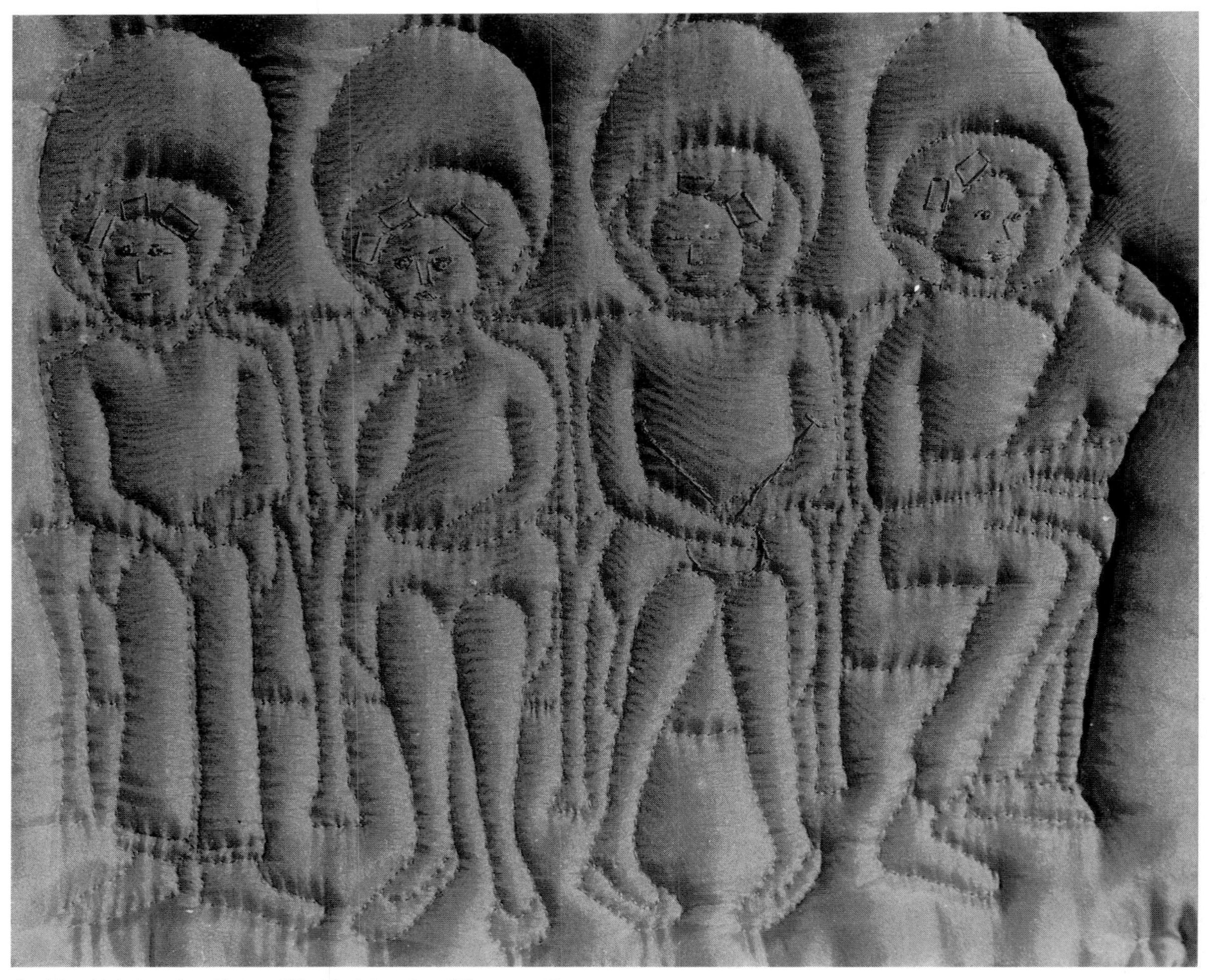

2 *The Hairdressing Salon. Wadded hand quilting on silk.*

3 *Functional quilting.*

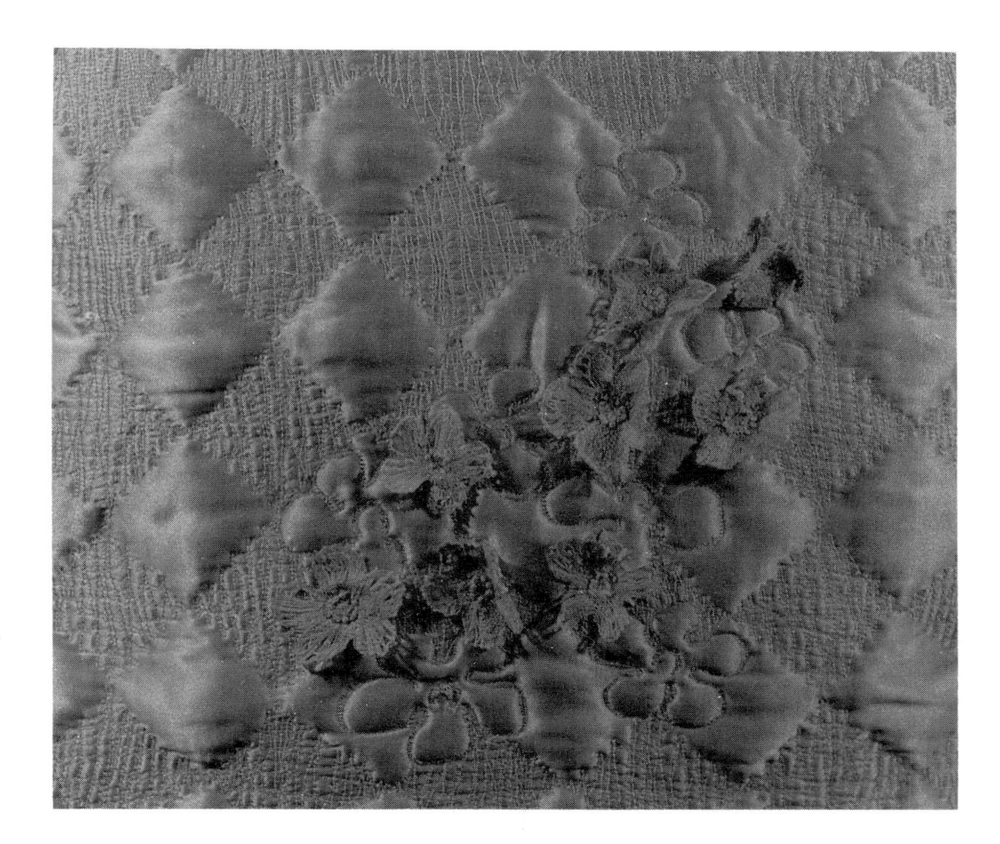

*4 Machine quilting on silk with applied machine embroidered flowers. (*Ann Farthing*)*

or the technique can be used to hold strips of wood or metal to form a flexible and protective material.

Trapunto quilting, or stuffed quilting (intermittent quilting in areas) This is a purely decorative form of quilting, where parts of the design stand out in sharp relief against the background. Two layers of fabric are stitched together in designs which form islands or enclosed areas and these are then padded out so that they form a raised surface.

Flat quilting Two layers of fabric are held together with stitches, giving an indented pattern on the surface.

Both historic and modern examples of all these variations can be seen in many museums and at exhibitions of contemporary embroidery and quilting.

All these methods can be intermixed and varied, particularly if the effect to be created is pictorial or decorative rather than practical. The variety of fabrics and materials used, and the type, colour and consistency of the fillings and stuffings, give a range of different and interesting impressions ranging from the conventional quilted surface which might be used for a jacket, to a fanciful wall hanging or some three-dimensional sculpture or construction. It is always important to remember that whatever is being made, the quilting pattern should be designed to fit into it.

For a beginner who has never quilted before, it is a good idea to work through some of the samples described in this book for each technique, using a variety of different fabrics and fillings as indicated then going on to try out your own ideas.

2

Wadded quilting, or English quilting

MATERIALS

Start with the most manageable fabrics in order to try out the technique. When this is mastered it is well worth experimenting on small samples of different fabrics, and combinations of fabrics and materials, because each gives an individual look, and some exciting effects can be achieved with unusual materials. Keep experiments for reference.

5 Wadded hand quilting on hand painted silk with patterns made by resist. (See colour plate 1.)

To begin, choose from the following materials.

Top layer Use a plain coloured woven fabric, e.g. silk, cotton, fine wool or wool and cotton mix, or any synthetic fabrics which feel soft and pliable like polyester cotton. Natural fabrics are easier to manage at first. The design should be marked out on the top fabric (see page 92).

Middle layer (wadding) Synthetic wadding is easily available and comes in different thicknesses. Choose a medium weight to begin, but go on to try out the thicker weights or use several layers of wadding. Cotton wadding is also available. It is sold folded and should be opened out and used with the fluffy side facing up. Any soft fabric like flannel, blanket or domette can be used. Each material gives a different finish ranging from almost flat to bouncy.

Bottom (backing) layer The fabric chosen depends on the function of the finished piece. If the bottom layer of fabric is to show as it might in a quilt or a jacket, it should match the top layer in colour and in fibre. In any case, the backing fabric should always be slightly firmer than the top layer, so that the puffy effect of the quilting can be seen on the surface and not underneath. Cotton polyester or cotton are suitable for fine wool or cotton, and muslin for silk.

6 Wadded quilting: the three layers.

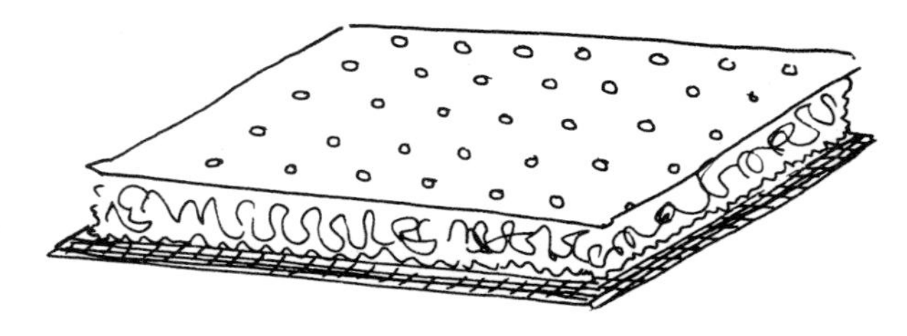

7 Wadded hand quilting on torn random dyed silk rectangles.

Thread Use sewing cotton (size 40) or cotton for topstitching or machine embroidery cotton (size 30) for cotton or wool or synthetic fabrics. Use silk twist on silk. If possible, use natural threads with natural fabrics and synthetic threads with synthetic fabrics. Traditionally the thread matches the background fabric, so that the indented pattern really stands out, but it is interesting to experiment with different coloured threads and yarns.

Embroidery frames and rings Quilting is much easier to do when the fabric is held in some sort of a frame and these range from the round tambour frames in various sizes which are used for small pieces of work to rectangular slate frames for more ambitious pieces, and large floor frames specially designed for quiltmaking.

Tambour frames of between 15 cm and 30 cm (6 in. and 12 in.) are a good size for practice pieces. A tambour frame has an inner ring which should be bound with tape before working, otherwise the wood is apt to tear the fabric. Use a wooden rather than a plastic frame. Many people use a frame made from canvas stretchers and these are both versatile and easy to use (see also page 91).

METHOD

1 Iron all fabrics.
2 Cut the top and the backing on the straight grain of the fabrics chosen. The backing needs to be slightly bigger than the top fabric, as this is held in the frame. The wadding should be the same size as the top fabric. Any materials likely to shrink should be washed first.
3 Mark out the design on the top fabric (see page 92).
4 Place the backing in the frame so that it is held taut and is not distorted. The wadding is then placed on the backing, with the top fabric covering it. Pin the four corners of the top fabric to the backing through the wadding. Starting in the centre, and working to the edges, tack the three materials firmly together with lines of stitches both across and down, about 5 cm (2 in.) apart. Remove the pins as they are pushed out of place by the stitches. Firm tacking is very important in quilting as the friction between fabrics and wadding can cause the

materials to move out of position, but make sure the tacking stitches themselves do not push the fabrics out of place.

5 Choose a matching thread and make a small knot. Give this a pull, so that it goes through the backing into the wadding where it will hold. To finish, work one or two small stitches and run the thread into the wadding. Make sure the thread is firmly anchored because it is annoying to find that it has come loose when the work is half done.

The stitches

These should not detract from the quilting pattern.

Running stitch worked in two movements, pushing the needle through then catching it at the back with the other hand and pushing it back, gives a good even stitch. Use a short sharp needle and short lengths of thread to prevent tangling, knotting or fraying caused by friction of the materials.

8 English quilting.

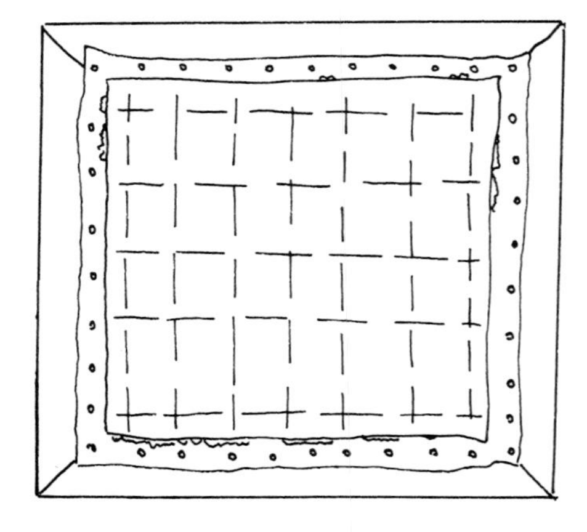

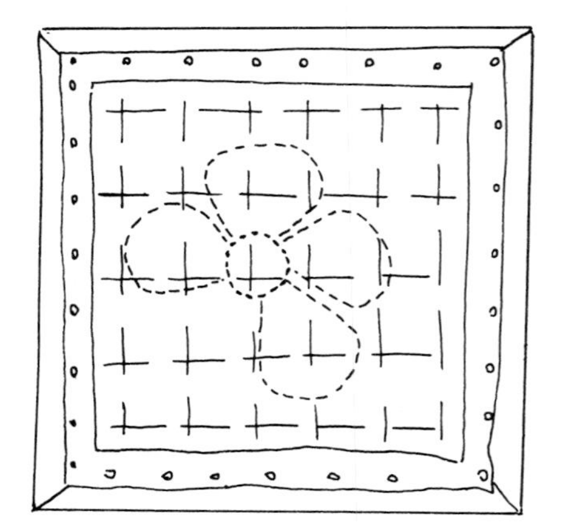

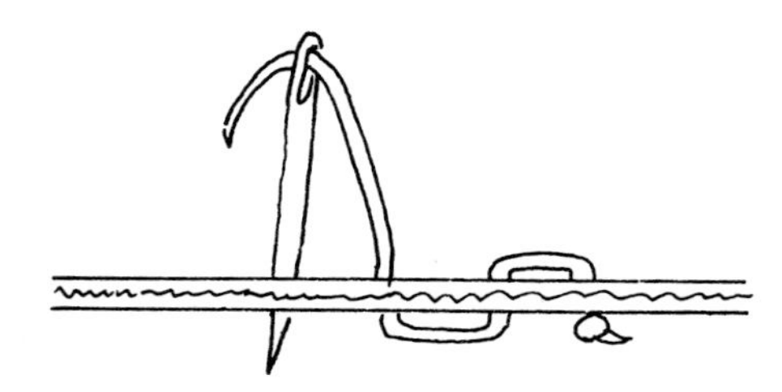

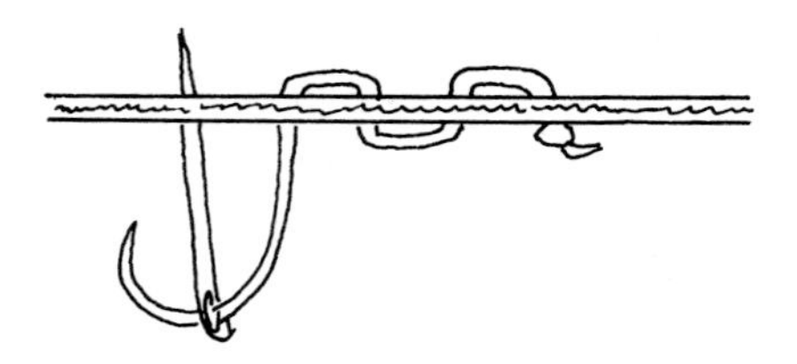

9 Running stitch.

Back stitch makes a more definite line. Other stitches which make definite lines might be used, e.g. chain stitch. The stitches need not be too small, but should be even.

Ties are sometimes used, and these should be tied correctly so that they do not slip. The effect of the quilting should be a dimpled, puffy surface.

10 Ties for wadded quilting.

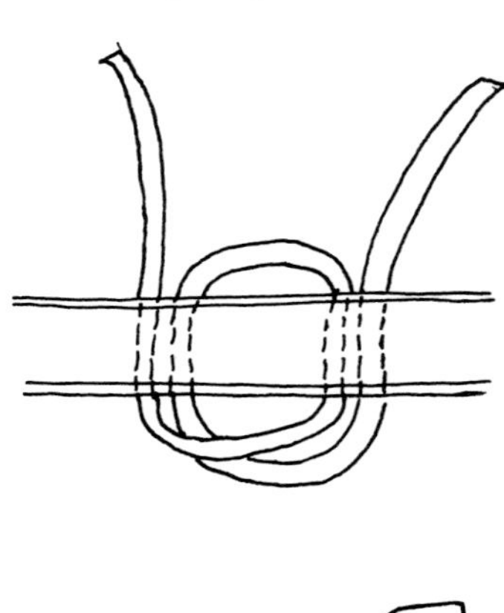

11 Tied quilting on hand painted silk. (See colour plate 2.)

12 Cushion by Elizabeth Woodthorpe. Machine quilting on hand dyed silk patchwork decorated with french knots and beads.

USING A SEWING MACHINE FOR QUILTING

Quilting by machine is not intended to replace hand quilting, but is a very useful addition to the effects which can be achieved with quilting techniques in general. The results are different from hand sewing, as the line of stitches gives a much firmer and harder finish which is very attractive in itself. Machine quilting is also very much quicker, and therefore larger things can be considered.

It is also useful to be able to combine hand and machine quilting. The sewing machine makes a continuous run of stitches, so the design for machine quilting should be chosen bearing this in mind. On a piece of any size it is often a good idea to use a mixture of controlled and free machine embroidery because layers of fabric stitched together with a machine will give a firm base for areas of free machine embroidery which can be added later.

Controlled machining

For practice, use the same types of material as were used for hand quilting. This time, though, the three layers should be cut the same size. Mark out the design on the right side of the top layer of fabric. All three layers should be firmly held together. Pinning is often more effective than tacking, as the machine is apt to move the tacking out of place. Sometimes you will find you have to use a combination of both. Place the pins at right angles to the line of sewing, but not quite touching. Do not use a frame.

The machine should be set for straight stitching with the top tension very slightly loosened, and the bottom tension normal. Stitch length should be medium to long.

Make texture and all-over pattern by stitching from one side of the work to the other, starting from alternate sides, either in lines or in criss-cross lines to make grid patterns, or stitch into the middle and back to the side. Base the patterns on straight or curved lines which the machine can manage easily. Zigzag patterns can also be used, but raise the machine foot every time you turn a corner.

The lines can be varied so that some are close together and some are far apart. Look at the spaces of the pattern as well as the lines.

Try to make each sample interesting in itself, either planning patterns on paper first or just doodling on the machine. Some of these designs will be suitable for hand quilting.

13 *Controlled machine quilting patterns.*

14 *Controlled machine quilting.*

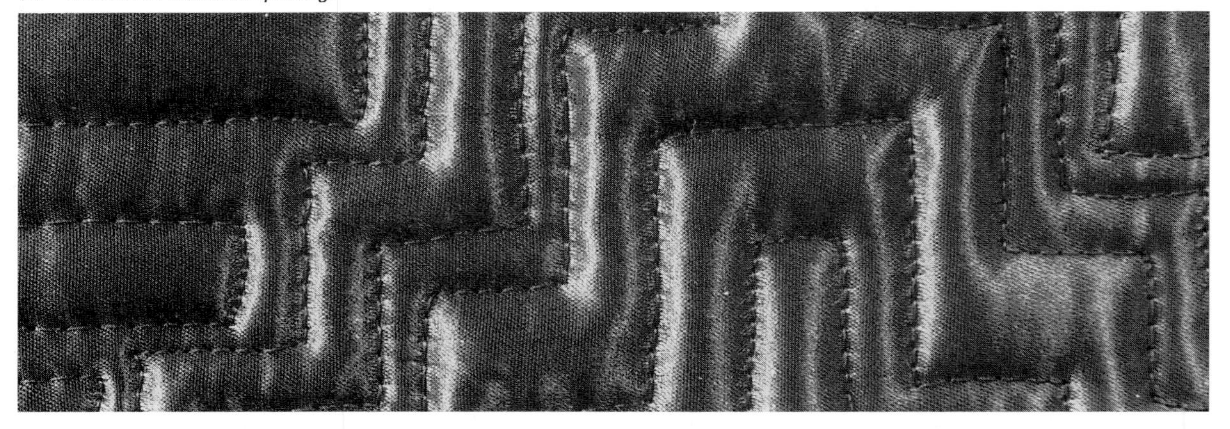

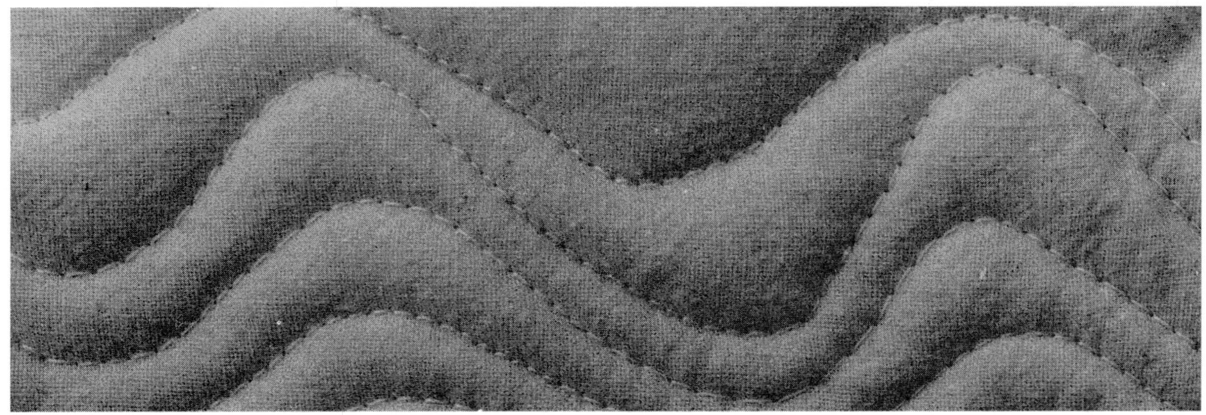

Free machine embroidery

Read the instructions in the machine manual and set up the machine for *machine embroidery* or for *darning*. Although machines are slightly different, the instructions are more or less the same. The idea is to ensure that the foot and the feed are put out of action to stop them pulling the fabric through the machine. This makes the machine sew on the spot and enables you to push the materials around beneath the needle and make patterns.

1 Remove the foot. Do not remove the needle bar unless it is necessary. Some machines respond better if fitted with an embroidery (darning) foot, as this gives more control and protection for the fingers.

2 Lower the feed. This is done on many machines by pressing a button. Some machines have a special plate to fit over the feed.

3 The work needs to be supported and held flat and taut, or it will be pushed out of shape and mangled up by the machine. Hold the fabric in a machine embroidery ring. If the fabric, wadding and backing are too bulky, the edges of the top and bottom layers only can be held in the ring, and the wadding will be held between. Fabric which has already been partly quilted by the controlled stitch method might be stiff enough without using a ring. A large picture or wall hanging can be supported on a stiff backing like paper-backed hessian, stiffened canvas fabric, etc. and will not need a ring.

4 Place the work under the needle. Put the foot in the *down* position. This is important, even though it is sometimes difficult to see if the needle bar is down when the foot has been removed.

5 Bring the bottom thread up to the surface, hold both threads, and with the needle almost touching the fabric start to sew. Cut the threads off after a few stitches. Keep the ring and materials flat on the base of the machine, just guiding them with the fingertips. Do not lift the ring towards the needle. Most machines have a removable table and this should be left in position to ensure a firm working surface. Drive smoothly and evenly. If your machine has a slow gear, it is a good idea to engage this.

Free machine embroidery is a technique which takes several hours to perfect, so keep practising. Doodle backwards and forwards and from side to side with straight and curved lines. There is no need to twist the frame or to lift the foot. You will find that you have more freedom to make much tighter curves, angles and shapes.

Using a sewing machine opens out many more possibilities for quilting patterns and there are numerous designs which can be used which are very easy to produce with simple equipment and very little skill in drawing.

15 Free machine quilting patterns.

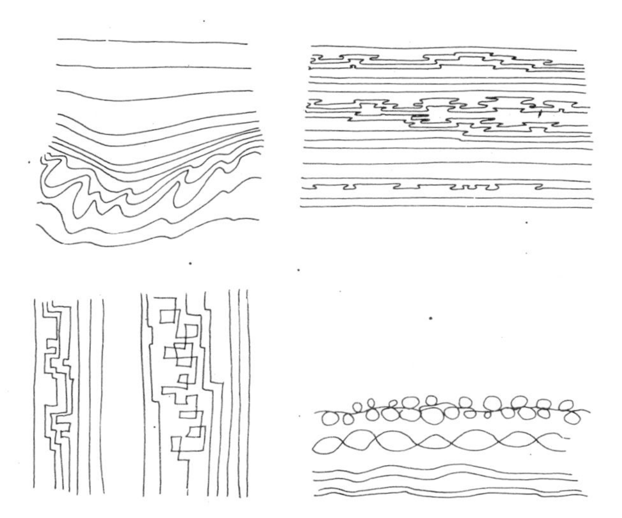

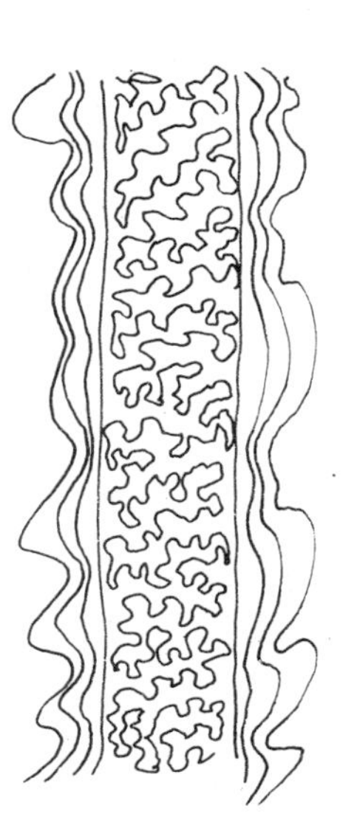

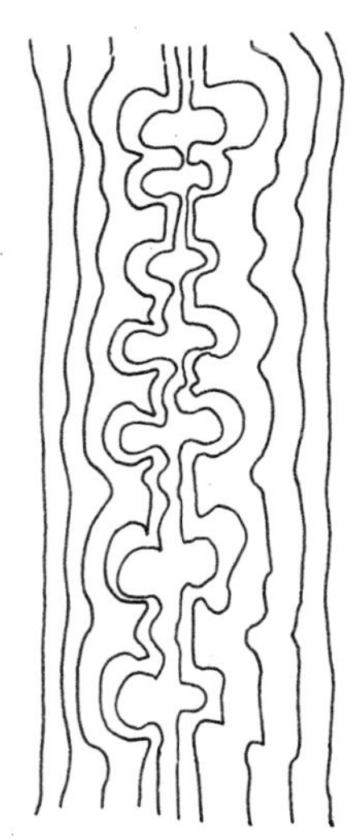

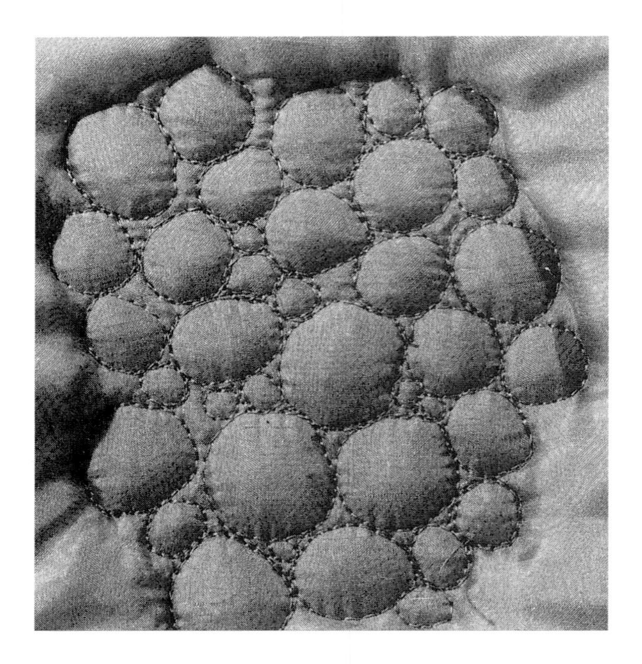

16 Free machine quilting.

DESIGNS FOR WADDED QUILTING

The patterns made by the stitches should be more or less evenly disposed over the surface so that the wadding is held in position, but not so close together that the beautiful raised surface texture is spoilt. Designs for quilting may be patterns and motifs made up of lines and geometric shapes, or they may be inspired by natural shapes and textures.

Patterns and motifs based on geometric shapes

Patterns of this sort are quite easy to do, and a study of old quilts will show that similar patterns have been used throughout history and in many different countries and regions.

Today, many people protest that they cannot draw, but it is doubtful whether most of the people who made quilts in the past could draw any better than the average modern embroiderer or craftsperson. However, although patterns were handed down from one generation to another, changed and added to, so that new patterns evolved, all of them could have been created simply by drawing round familiar household articles like cups, glasses and plates. By using a straight edge with the circular pattern produced or by folding and cutting paper shapes in various ways, it is possible to create all sorts of geometric shapes. These can then be arranged to form motifs and repeated to make all-over patterns and border patterns that are ideal for quilting. Although some modern geometric patterns used for quilting look different from the more traditional designs, this is only because of the way the basic shapes are arranged.

17 Border designs.

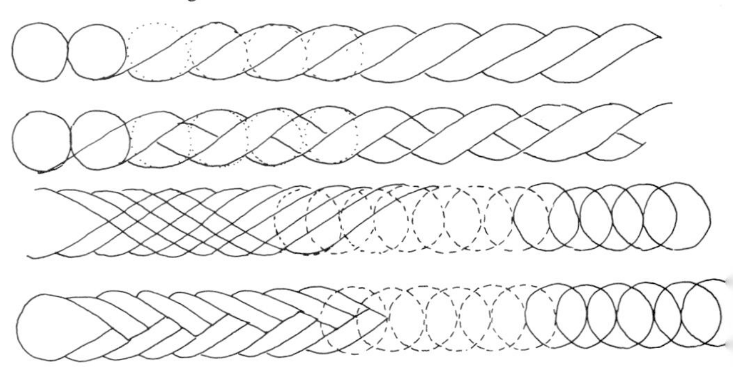

18 Developments of the circle.

a)

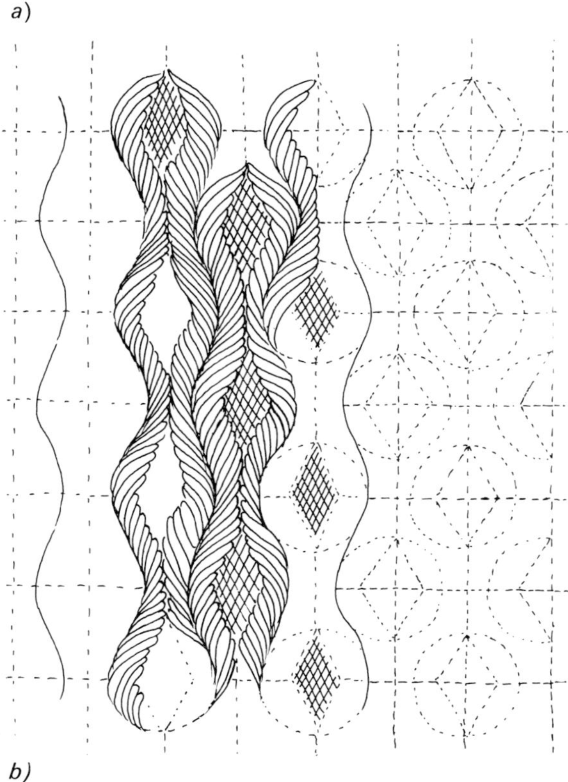

b)

19 Durham Quilt. Quilts were made by families around the British Isles right up to the Second World War. The quilt illustrated here was made in Bishop Auckland and presented to the Revd William Soper Liddle on the occasion of his marriage to Kathleen Kingsnorth in 1936. Revd Liddle is now 86 years old, but he remembers when quilts were made by whole families, including the children. His own father was a miner. For several nights a family would sit round the trestle which supported the quilt, and work on it together. He remembers the '... modest little houses, but there was a feeling of comfort and pride in adding to the home. Sometimes a quilt was given to a bridal couple – no insubstantial present at that time.' The quilt is still used by his son's family. The quilt aptly illustrates that designs were based on simple geometric shapes.

(a) The quilt.

(b) The middle panel based on circles on a grid pattern. Notice how the curved lines and feathers are formed by using the circles as a foundation.

(c) The border pattern made by interlocking circles.

(d) The corner patterns.

c)

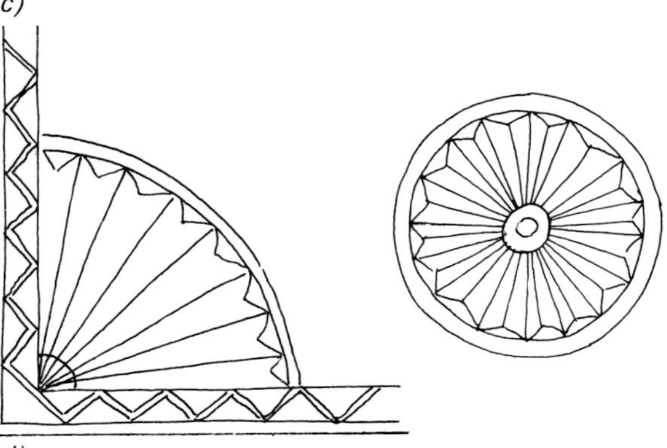

d)

Look at the traditional patterns of British and American quilts at a local museum. Notice how most quilts are made up of three basic elements:

- Motifs or spots of pattern – these can range from a decorated circle or rectangle to something much more complicated like a bowl of fruit or flowers.
- Border patterns all round the edge and dividing up the central areas into more manageable spaces.
- All-over interlocking patterns used as background and to fill in shapes.

Try to analyse the basic shapes used to make the individual patterns and notice how these patterns have been combined to fit into an area. The finished quilt might look quite involved at first sight but, broken down into its component parts, the pattern is often based upon one or two simple shapes like circles and squares, rectangles and triangles.

Using the circle as a basis for design

It is interesting to experiment to see how many patterns can be made using a simple shape like a circle. Either draw round something with a circular rim, like a wineglass, or use a pair of compasses and make a template with mounting board. It is also possible to buy a plastic template with circles cut into it at a graphics supplies shop.

Interlocking or all-over patterns

Make a block pattern of circles. You will find that it is possible either to draw the circles underneath one another, or in a staggered pattern like a brick wall. Draw both arrangements.

The circles can also be drawn overlapping, making different patterns and forming more shapes. As you draw and new pattern shapes emerge, isolate these and repeat them to form yet more patterns.

Draw accurately and carefully, so that the edges of the circles just touch one another. At this stage it is a good idea to have the basic patterns photocopied, so that you have plenty of spare copies to work on.

Go over these copies with coloured pencils, pens or paint, elaborating on the basic pattern, filling in some spaces, doubling some lines. The patterns created might be either regular or irregular but are held together by the grid of circles.

Go back to the two basic blocks of circles, and, using a ruler, draw a grid of straight lines along the edges of the circles to make a mesh. Go on to draw

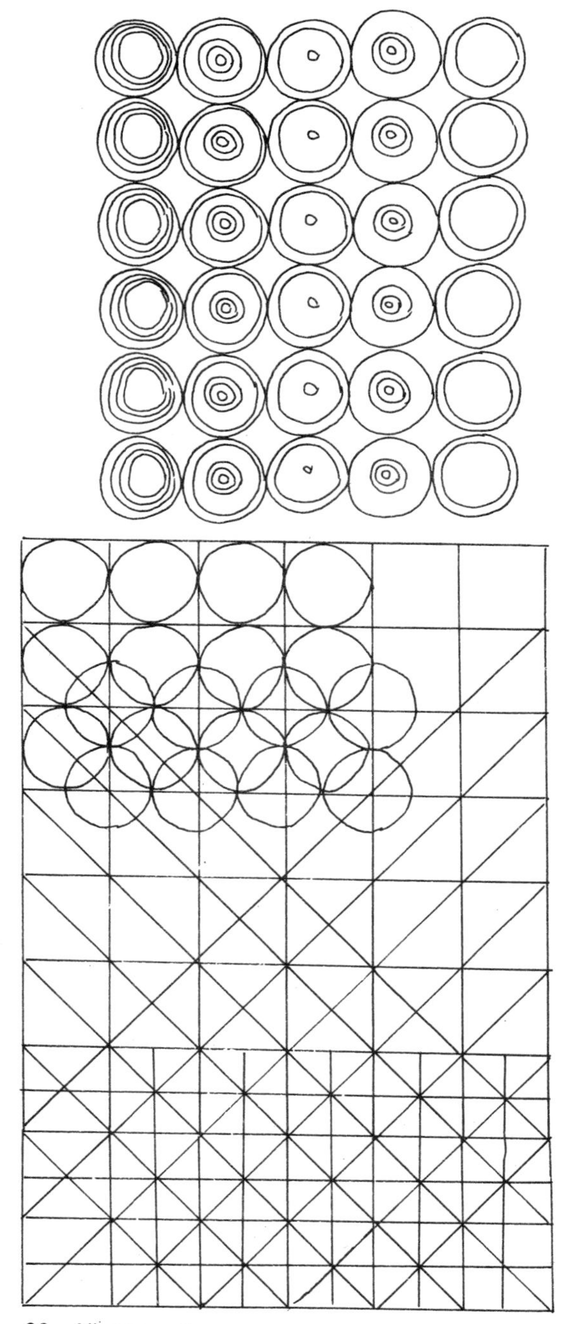

20 *All-over pattern.*

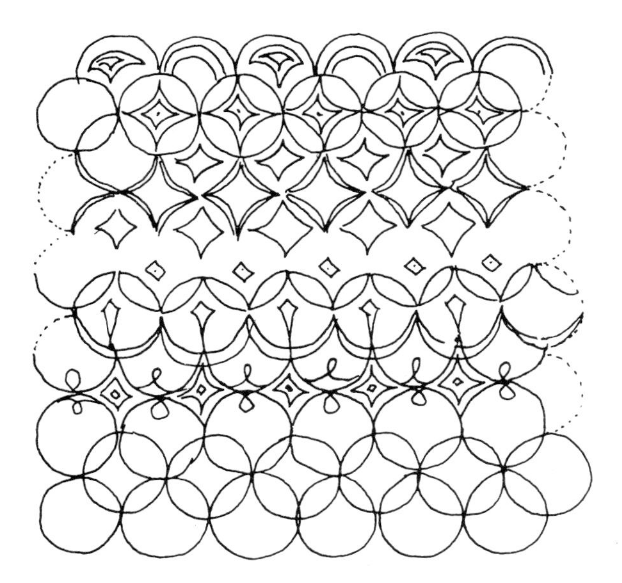

If you draw the basic circle patterns in faint pencil and the lines in ink or felt-tip pen, the grid patterns can be photocopied and only the straight lines will show. Use the grid for creating more elaborate patterns.

Areas of pattern can also be picked out and used by themselves as spots of decoration or motifs.

Motifs using individual geometric shapes

Up to now all the patterns created have been based on a regular arrangement of circles. However, circles of different sizes can also be used to create a motif pattern.

Cut out a number of circles in three different sizes, small, medium and large. Arrange them in a regular pattern. Some might overlap, or be contained within others. Try to make the arrangement look balanced and attractive. When you are satisfied, draw round the shapes.

Practise drawing this sort of circle pattern freehand. Freehand drawing and cutting out gives much more spontaneity, and templates are apt to be restrictive. Any patterns used for a particular function can be drawn out more carefully if necessary.

Using a similar range of circles, make a series of irregular patterns, where the circles are arranged as if they have been splattered. Allow smaller shapes to dribble off towards the edge.

A motif can also be designed by using the same variety of circles but this time arranged within a large circle. The pattern might be regular or irregular.

21 Motifs within the all-over pattern.

22 Motifs developed from circles.

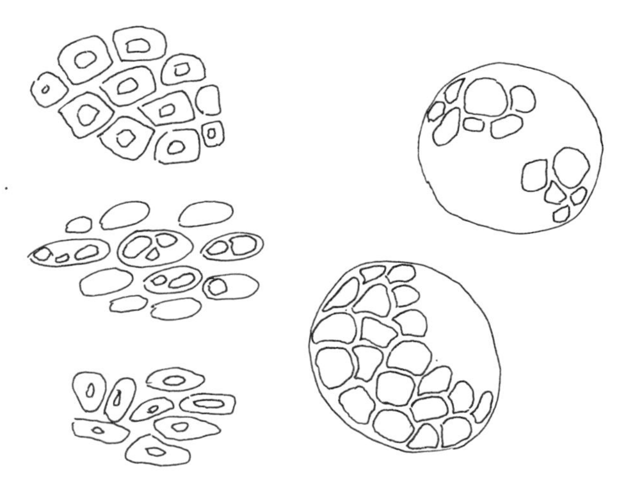

Border patterns

Make a linear pattern by arranging circles of various sizes in a border. Like the patterns above, the borders might be made up of circles of different size, circles which overlap or circles which enclose one another. Always balance the shapes against each other to make a pleasing arrangement.

23 Geometric borders.

the diagonals, which will go through the centres of the circles. It immediately becomes clear that the two basic arrangements of circles produce two different grid patterns, one based on squares and the other on triangles and diamonds.

Variations

- A large number of interlocking patterns, borders and motifs can be created by making patterns in a similar way with other regular geometric shapes like rectangles, triangles and diamonds.
- Patchwork templates can also be used to make a basic pattern which can then be further decorated with lines.
- Many of the patterns will be enhanced by adding lines, either following the edge of the

24 Designs developed from geometric shapes and lines.

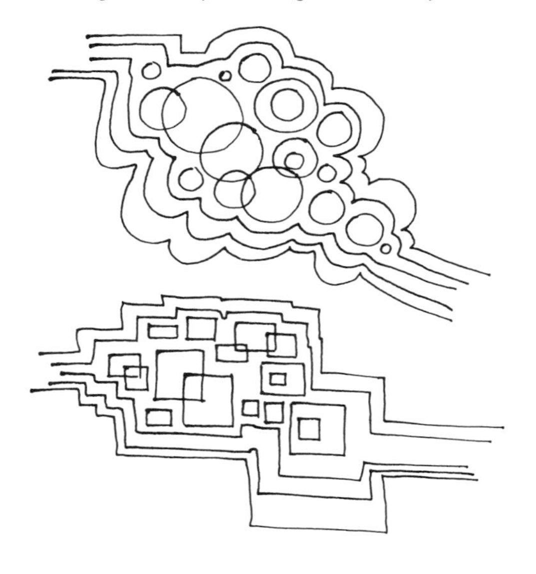

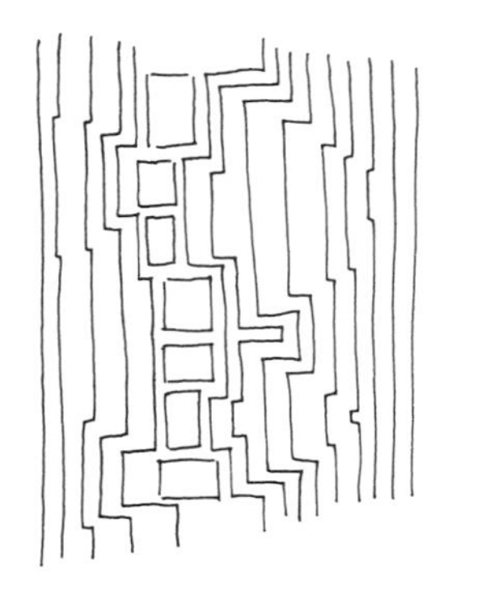

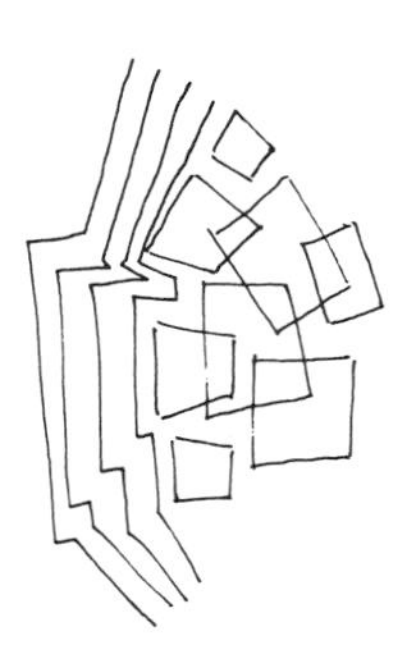

25 Designs using familiar shapes.

pattern formed by the shapes, or within some of the shapes themselves.

- Use very simple domestic shapes like cake cutters or the shapes from a child's wooden puzzle or a baby's plastic letters. Look for leaf or shell shapes or fan shapes which can be repeated easily over an area.

It is not a good idea to mix too many individual shapes, or the design will become too complicated, but just two sets of shapes used together, e.g. circles and squares, or rectangles and triangles, etc. make interesting and beautiful patterns.

Try out each idea at least half a dozen times to get into the rhythm of designing. Be willing to be sidetracked by other ideas which might occur to you. With very little effort, you can see that a variety of patterns can be created, some of which might look like traditional patterns, while one or two might be completely original.

At the same time, make a collection of similar patterns from the environment, not only from other quilted articles which might be seen in exhibitions or museums, but also in wood, metal and stone, in patterns on book covers, in fabrics and wallpapers, and so on. These can be kept in a folder with your original designs and used as reference material.

Choose some of the motifs or patterns you have designed, to try out the technique of wadded quilting, both by hand and on the machine. If the pattern is too big or too small, it will have to be enlarged or reduced.

Many of these designs will be suitable for the other techniques described in this book and also for other embroidery techniques. Have the confidence to use your own designs. Many people feel that their designs are inferior, but this is usually because they have worked on them so much that they have become over-critical.

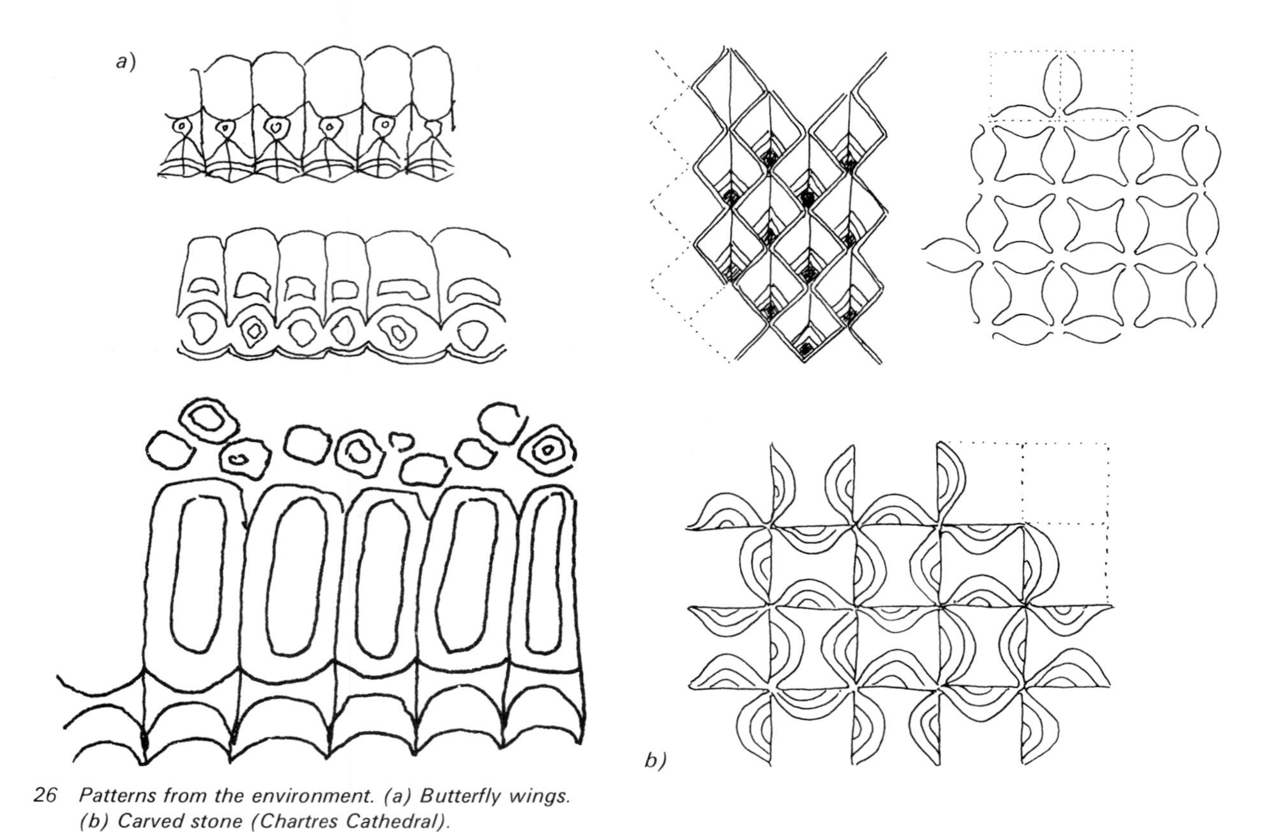

26 *Patterns from the environment. (a) Butterfly wings. (b) Carved stone (Chartres Cathedral).*

27 *Dividing a square in different ways. Mondrian, the artist, developed this idea in his abstract paintings.*

3

Trapunto quilting, or stuffed quilting

This method of quilting makes use of two layers of fabric but without a layer of wadding between. The wadding or stuffing is added later, but only in some areas of the design, so that the quilting is intermittent rather than all over. Because of this, trapunto quilting is not normally used for warmth and protection, but only for decoration.

MATERIALS

Choose from the following materials to try out the technique of trapunto quilting.

Top layer Use a soft smooth fabric like cotton,

28 French Scene by Maggie Jones. Trapunto and corded quilting on calico.

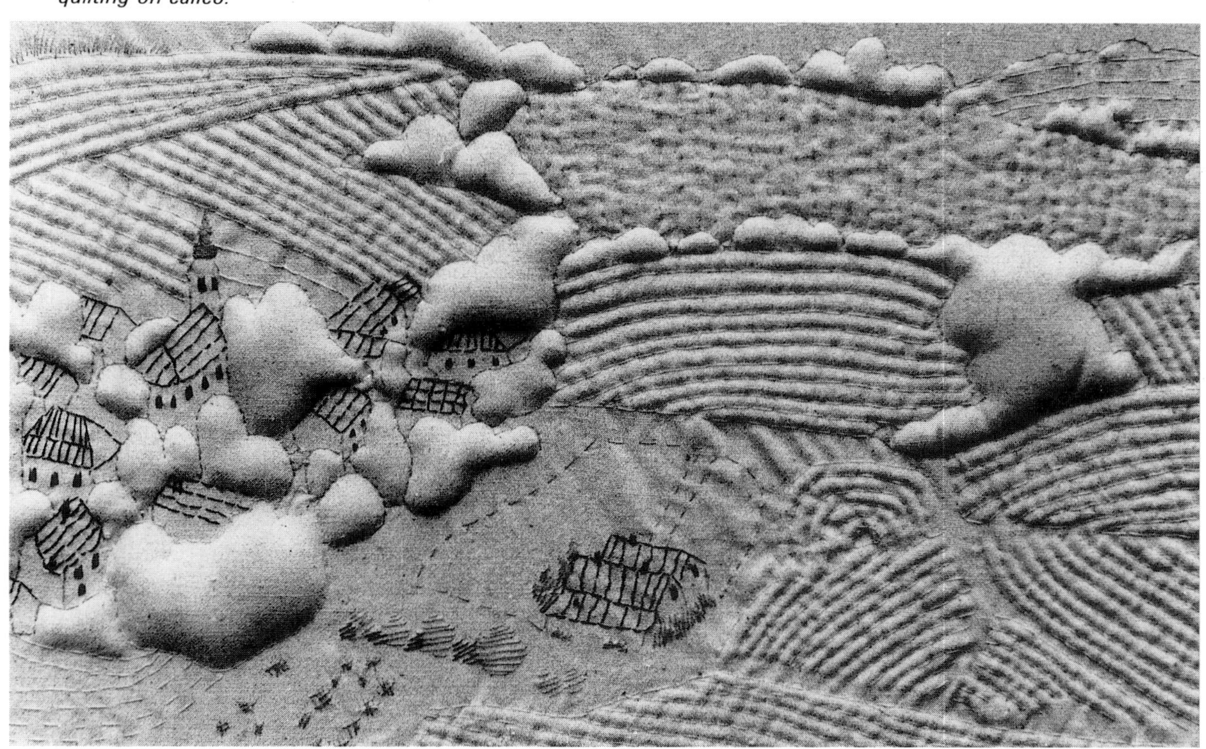

29 Trapunto quilting.

silk or a fine wool/cotton mix.

Bottom layer Use muslin, linen scrim or some loosely woven fabric. As the whole idea of this technique is to throw parts of the design into relief, fabrics need to be chosen carefully to make sure that the bumps are on the surface and not underneath. For this reason something like polycotton might be a better choice for some designs. In any case, always try out a variety of fabrics before starting on a large project and keep samples for reference.

This technique can be carried out by hand or machine, or a mixture of both. As in wadded quilting it is much easier to use a frame to hold the fabrics together while you are working. If this is not possible, perhaps because the work is too big or bulky, the materials should be pinned together securely.

The design for trapunto quilting must be made up of areas which are enclosed, so that the stuffing is held in one place to form islands of raised surface texture. The padded surface areas can be used to emphasize the design.

HAND METHOD

1 Iron both top and bottom fabrics and if possible have the grain of the fabrics running the same way. You might find later, in more experimental work with knits, for instance, that this is not possible.

30 Trapunto quilting by machine. Fabric crayon design on Terylene.

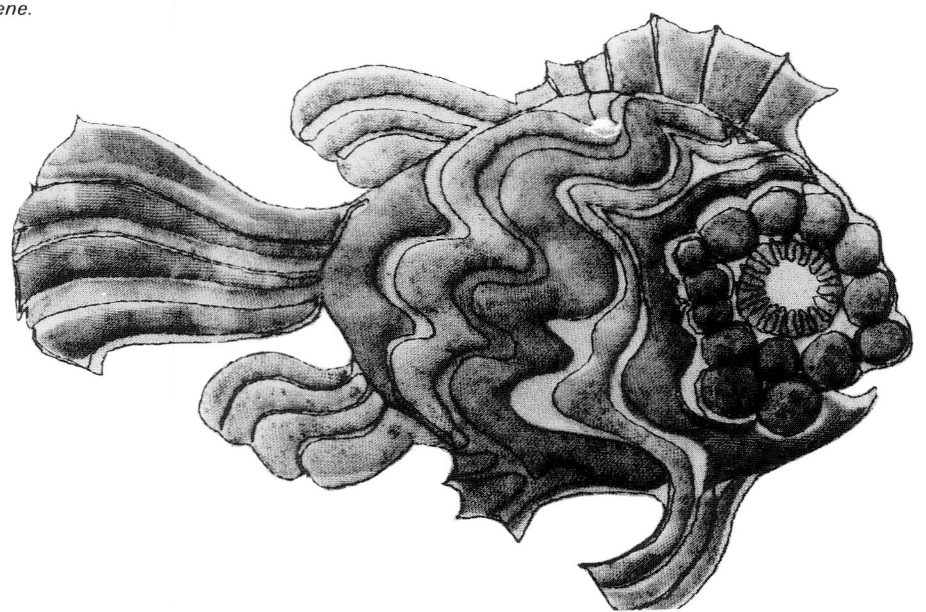

2 Mark out the design on the top fabric. If necessary the design can be marked on the backing.
3 Tack the two fabrics together by laying the backing on a flat surface and placing the top fabric over it, so that there are no creases. Frame up the fabric, making sure the design is not pulled out of shape.
4 Sew along the lines of the design, using back stitch. Start with a knot and a single back stitch, and finish off securely, as the stitches will be under some strain.
5 Turn the work to the back. With a stiletto or a large blunt needle, part the fibres and push in wadding or stuffing to pad out the shape. If the backing fabric is not loosely woven, cut a small slit with sharp scissors, and push in padding. It is important to sew up the slit to create the right effect.

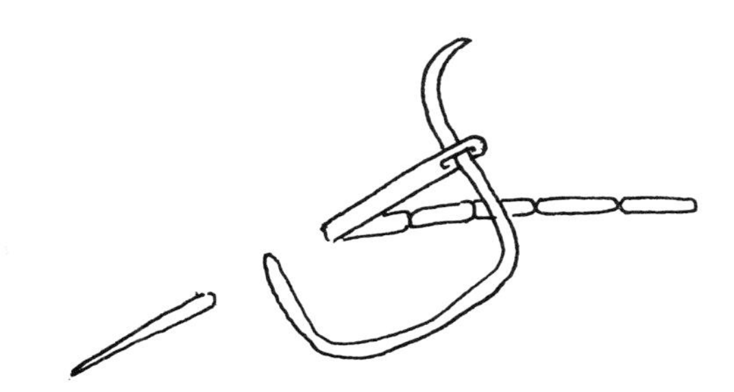

31 Back stitch.

MACHINE METHOD

Results of doing trapunto quilting on a machine are excellent, either with straight machining where a ring will be unnecessary, or with free machine embroidery, where you will need a ring.

Plan a design where you exploit the fact that the machine makes a continuous line. It is very annoying to have to start and finish off repeatedly, and interrupts the flow. It does not matter if you go over some lines more than once. With controlled machining, patterns with criss-cross lines which go right from one edge of the fabric to the other are particularly useful.

Trapunto quilting can be allied with wadded quilting to accentuate parts of a design. Work the trapunto quilting first, then go on to quilt as already described.

PATTERNS AND MOTIFS BASED ON NATURAL DESIGNS

If you take a magnifying glass and look at the pattern on a cabbage leaf, a corn on the cob or the seedhead of a sunflower, it seems as if nature is mocking some of the tight little formal grid patterns we manage to make with a ruler and pencil. None of the shapes is exactly the same, none of the angles is true and like a very old house which is slowly sinking back into the ground, the whole thing is slightly off-key. Interlocking patterns seem to have been nudged and pushed so that each individual shape which goes to make the whole is unique, slightly different from the rest, but still holding together to make a pleasing whole.

Examine objects like seedheads, lichen-covered stones, leaves and so on through a magnifying glass, or take a look at almost any natural material through a microscope, if you can get hold of one. Make a collection of natural interlocking shapes. Try to draw some of these, looking particularly at the shapes which make up the pattern. If you prefer, these can be cut or torn out of paper and stuck down.

You can also take photographs. An ordinary camera, moved as close as possible to the subject, can produce very useful photos. Flash is apt to flatten shadows, and the natural light on a sunny day is often more successful. If you have a single lens reflex camera with a close-up lens, or tubes, you can take photographs as near as 8 cm (3 in.).

When the film is developed, have some of the photographs photocopied. Some may be suitable for further enlargement on a photocopier. You can then trace the main lines and shapes on the photocopy, trying to simplify the tracing into a collection of shapes. Keep referring back to the photograph and to the original.

These natural shapes and patterns can be collected, either as sketches or photographs, and used as a basis for trapunto quilted designs. All or just some of the shapes can be padded so that they stand out in relief against the background. Remember: *shape* is one of the most important aspects of design in quilting.

32 *Natural designs for trapunto.*

33 *Cushion by Elizabeth Woodthorpe. The design was taken from a microscope slide of a transverse section of marram grass. Wadded machine quilting with reverse appliqué and hand embroidery.*

4

Corded quilting, or Italian quilting

In Italian quilting, lines are created and quilted by working parallel lines of stitches, either by hand or machine. The channels formed are then threaded with a quilting yarn, so that they stand out in relief against the background. There are two methods of doing this.

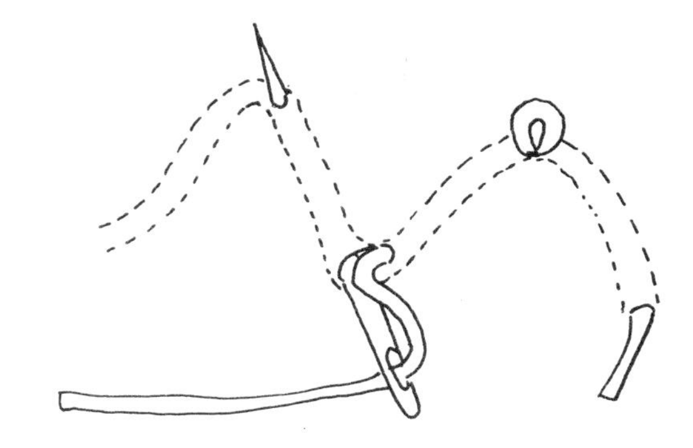

35 Corded quilting, method A.

34 Belt by Elizabeth Woodthorpe. Hand worked corded quilting in black silk decorated with beads. The design was based on a leaf from a Swiss cheese plant.

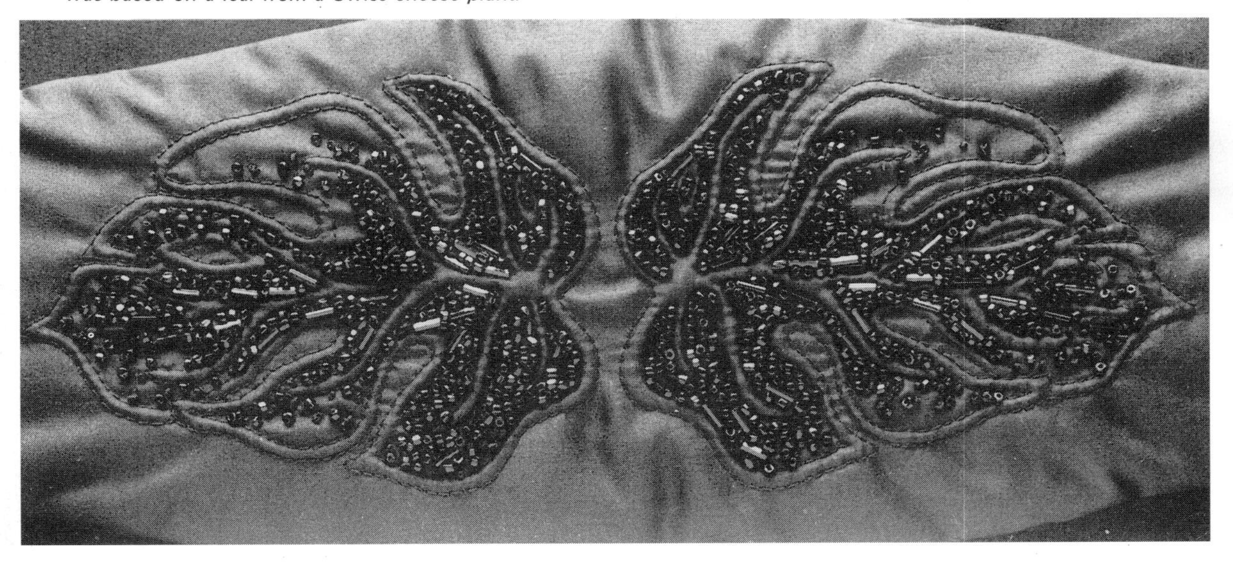

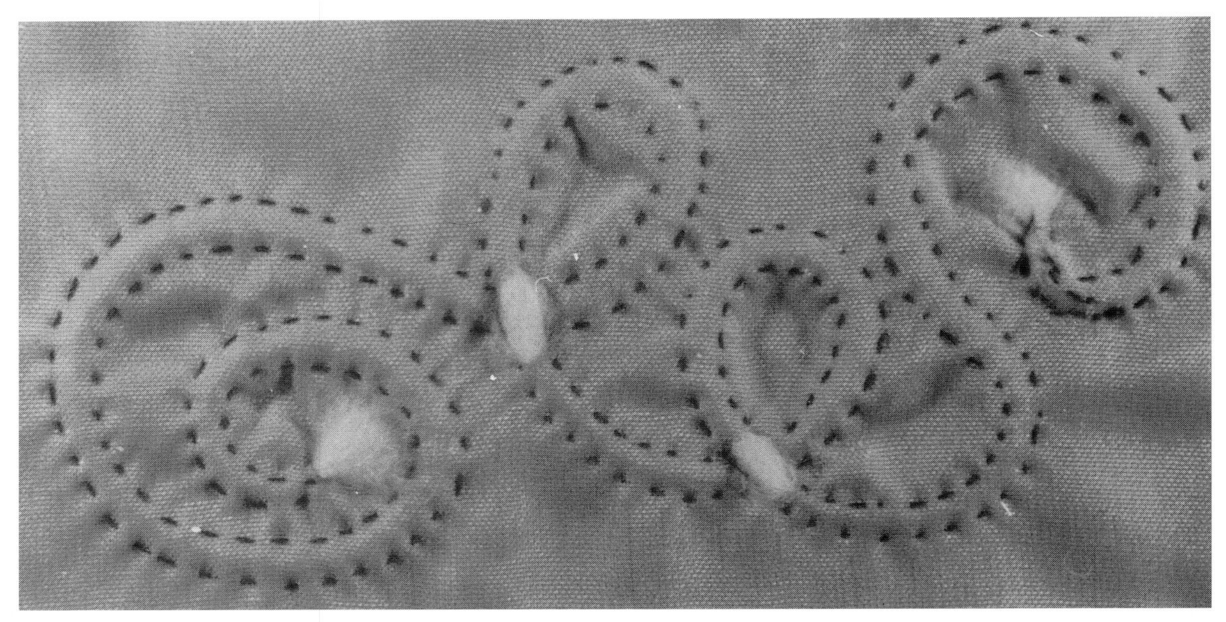

36 Corded quilting, method A: reverse side.

METHOD A

Materials

Top layer To try out the technique, use a soft smooth fabric like cotton, silk, fine wool mix, etc.
Bottom layer The bottom fabric should be chosen so that the relief appears on the surface of the fabric and not underneath. Muslin or cheesecloth, organdie or polycotton might be used.

Mark out the design on either the top fabric or the underside of the bottom fabric. Carefully pin the fabrics together.

Use an embroidery ring to hold the fabrics flat, but do not pull the fabric out of shape or the design will be distorted.

Use running stitch or back stitch to work along the lines of the design. Make sure the thread is tightly anchored both at the beginning and at the end of the work.

The quilting yarn A specialist quilting yarn is manufactured and can usually be obtained by mail order from specialist suppliers. A double knitting wool gives a soft line, or for a more definite line use piping cord or string. The quilting yarn should fit snugly into the channel, and it is worth experimenting before starting anything large to make sure that the quilting yarn is not so thick that it is bursting out, but not so thin that it makes no real impression. If the channel is wide, it might be necessary to double or quadruple the quilting thread so that it pads out the line in a satisfactory way.

Turn the work over and thread the quilting yarn through the channels from the back of the work. If you use something loosely woven like muslin for the backing, you can part the threads as in trapunto quilting, but otherwise make a hole with a stiletto or a thick needle.

At any intersections, where one line of the design crosses another, bring the needle out through the backing and cross on the *outside*. In any case you will need to keep bringing the needle out on the wrong side to pull the quilting yarn along. Always go back through the same hole. Similarly, at a sharp corner bring the quilting yarn to the outside and leave a little loop of yarn, so that the corner looks really sharp from the right side.

METHOD B

Use one layer of fabric which should be held in a frame. Mark out the design, then holding the quilting wool at the back of the fabric, work double back stitch on the front of the fabric between the parallel lines of the design. The quilting wool is caught by the stitches at the back and held in place. Back the quilting with another fabric.

37 Corded quilting, method B: double back stitch.

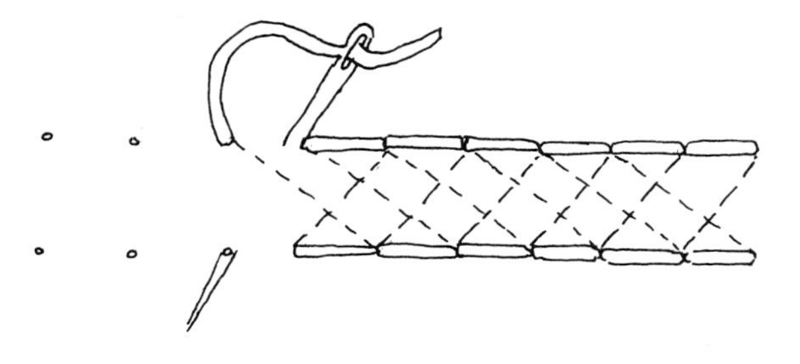

DESIGNING PATTERNS FOR CORDED QUILTING

Patterns can be made from some of the cut paper patterns suggested in Chapter 1 on wadded quilting. Take a pattern and draw round it, then draw another line parallel to the first and about 5 mm ($\frac{1}{4}$ in.) to the outside.

38 Designs for corded quilting.

Corded quilting can be seen at its best when it is used for some of the beautiful and complicated interlocking patterns similar to the Celtic knots seen in illuminated manuscripts and used in decorations on Moorish artefacts. Although at first sight these patterns and knots look almost impossible to design, they are all based on simple shapes and lines which have been complicated with added loops and curlicues. If the lines of the design are then doubled and interlocked, the result looks tortuous.

Try this by starting very simply, then building up to more complicated designs. Many designs can be found in books on pattern and design. Look out for suitable patterns on stonework and some wood carvings.

1 Using a pencil, lightly draw two overlapping curved lines.

2 Lightly draw a line parallel to the first to make a double line.

3 Interlock the lines, by following one double line and taking it under at the first intersection, over at the second, and so on, in strict rotation.

4 Go over the design with a black pen.

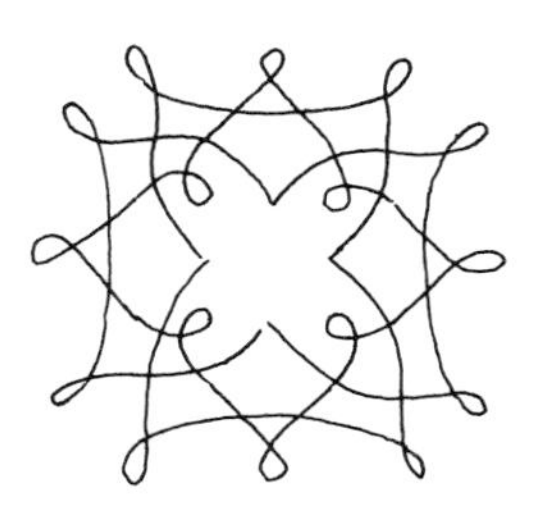

Continue to make linear patterns by making regular curved overlapping lines, adding loops if they will fit in comfortably, then doubling and interlocking. It soon becomes obvious that you have to be accurate and that you have to make sure that there is enough room to double the lines without spoiling the design.

Make use of circles, compasses, French curves and similar drawing aids. Geometric shapes can also be superimposed to form motifs and borders, then the lines can be doubled and interlocked. Start simply by using combinations of regular geometric shapes, e.g. a cross over a circle, a circle over a square, etc. If you intend to use a shape more than once, make an accurate stencil out of card or trace it off a master drawing.

Patterns can also be drawn from a centre line, so that one side mirrors the other. You will need tracing paper and a sharp pencil.

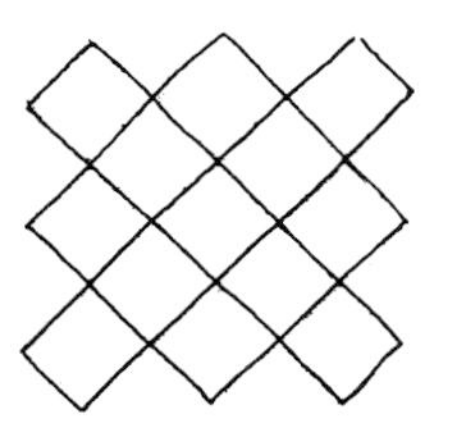

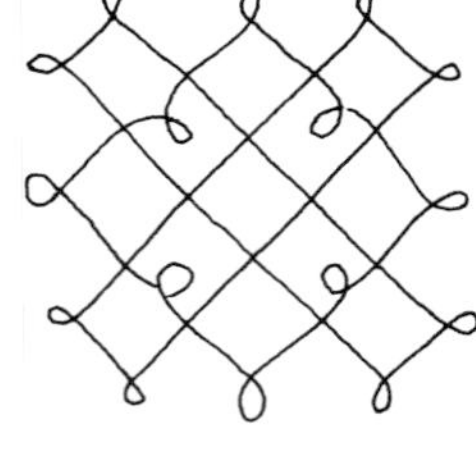

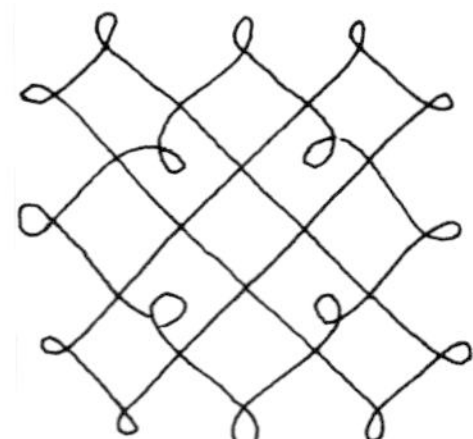

39 Developing a design for corded quilting.

40 Corded quilting patterns. Some of these are based on carved stone designs (Bristol Cathedral).

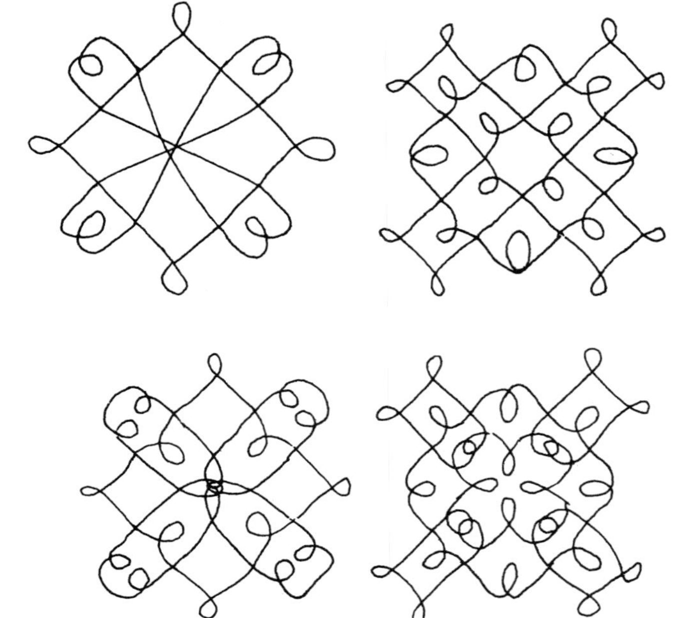

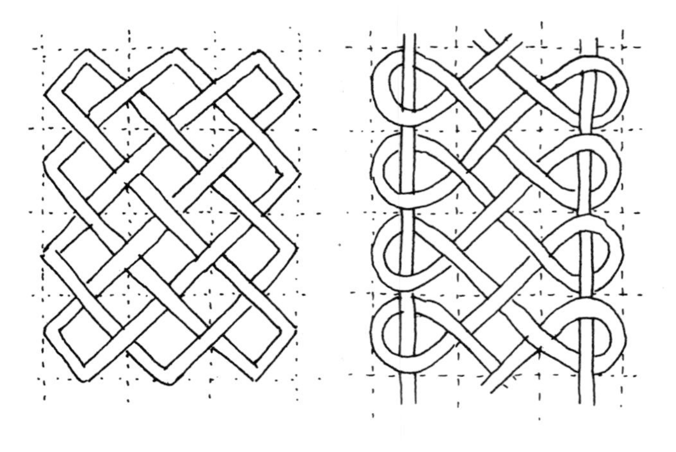

1 Draw a vertical line.
2 Draw a curved line with loops, from the top of the line, out to one side, and coming back to the bottom of the line.
3 Mirror this line on the opposite side, by folding the paper in half and tracing through.
4 Double the lines and interlock.
Draw these lines lightly, as lines are built one over another. Use a sharp hard pencil. Finally, go over the finished design with a thin black pen. These designs can be enlarged most accurately on a photocopier.

CORDED QUILTING ON A SEWING MACHINE

A sewing machine will sew a straight or slightly curved line and it is easy to make a line parallel to the first, because the foot can be used as a guide. The more curved the line, the more inaccurate its parallel is likely to be. A twin needle can be used for narrow lines.

One of the beauties of machine corded quilting is that if you stick to designs made up of straight and angled lines, it is very easy to do, and the fabric created is both beautiful and interesting. It is also flexible, supple and quite hardwearing. It you look at old corsets in museums, you will see that they are machine corded in straight-line patterns, and – instead of being threaded with yarn – whalebone or even strips of wood and metal are used to add stiffness. Some of these old corsets are almost works of art themselves.

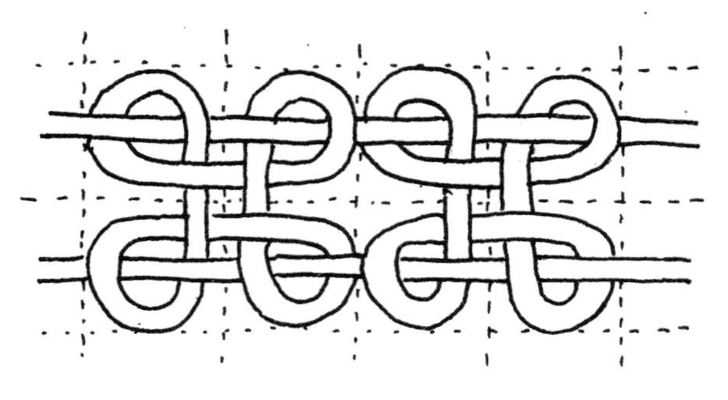

1 ▲ The fabric was divided into areas by lines of resist medium, and some areas were painted with resist patterns. The whole was then painted in different colours. Quilting follows the lines of resist.

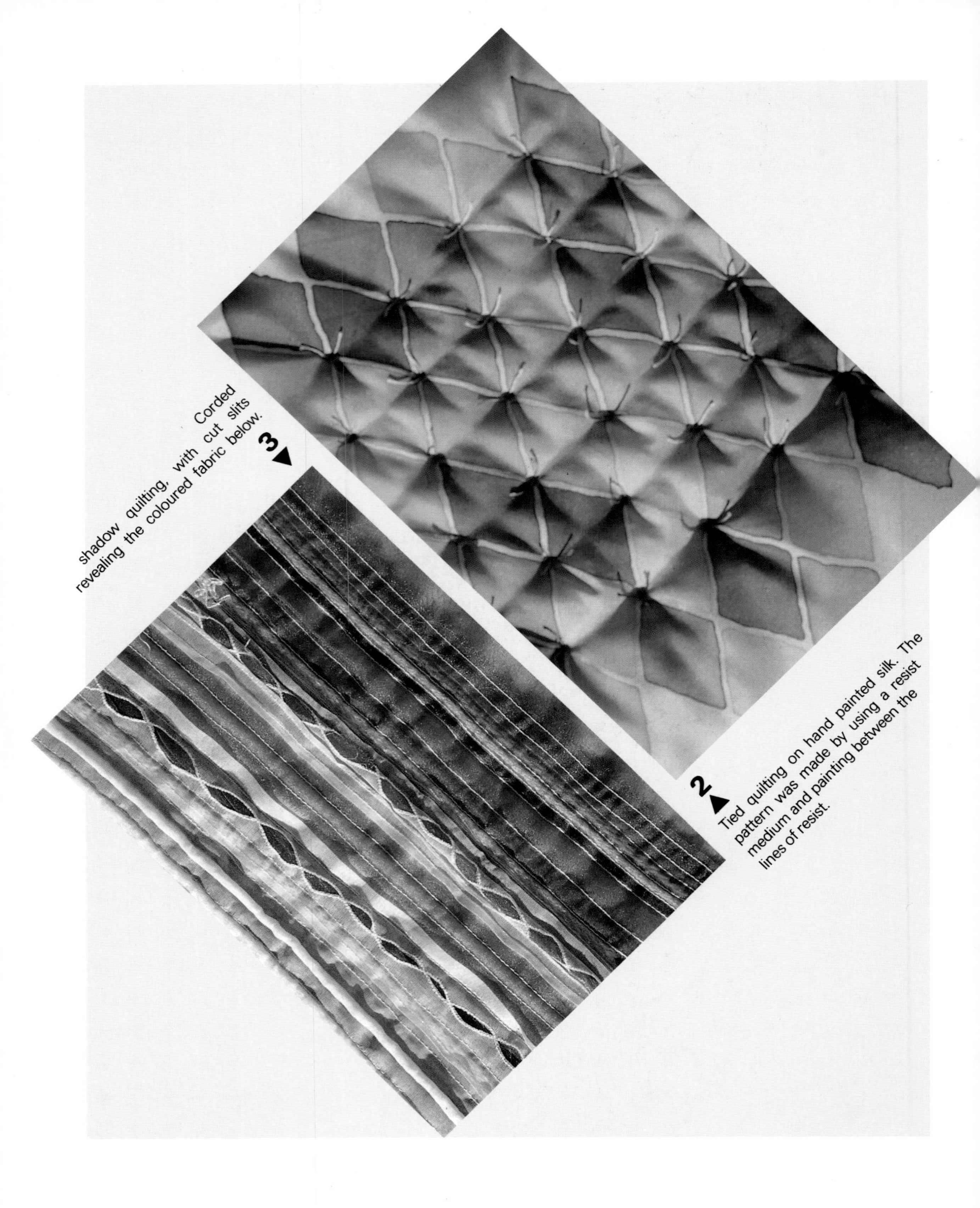

3▼ Corded shadow quilting, with cut slits revealing the coloured fabric below.

2▲ Tied quilting on hand painted silk. The pattern was made by using a resist medium and painting between the lines of resist.

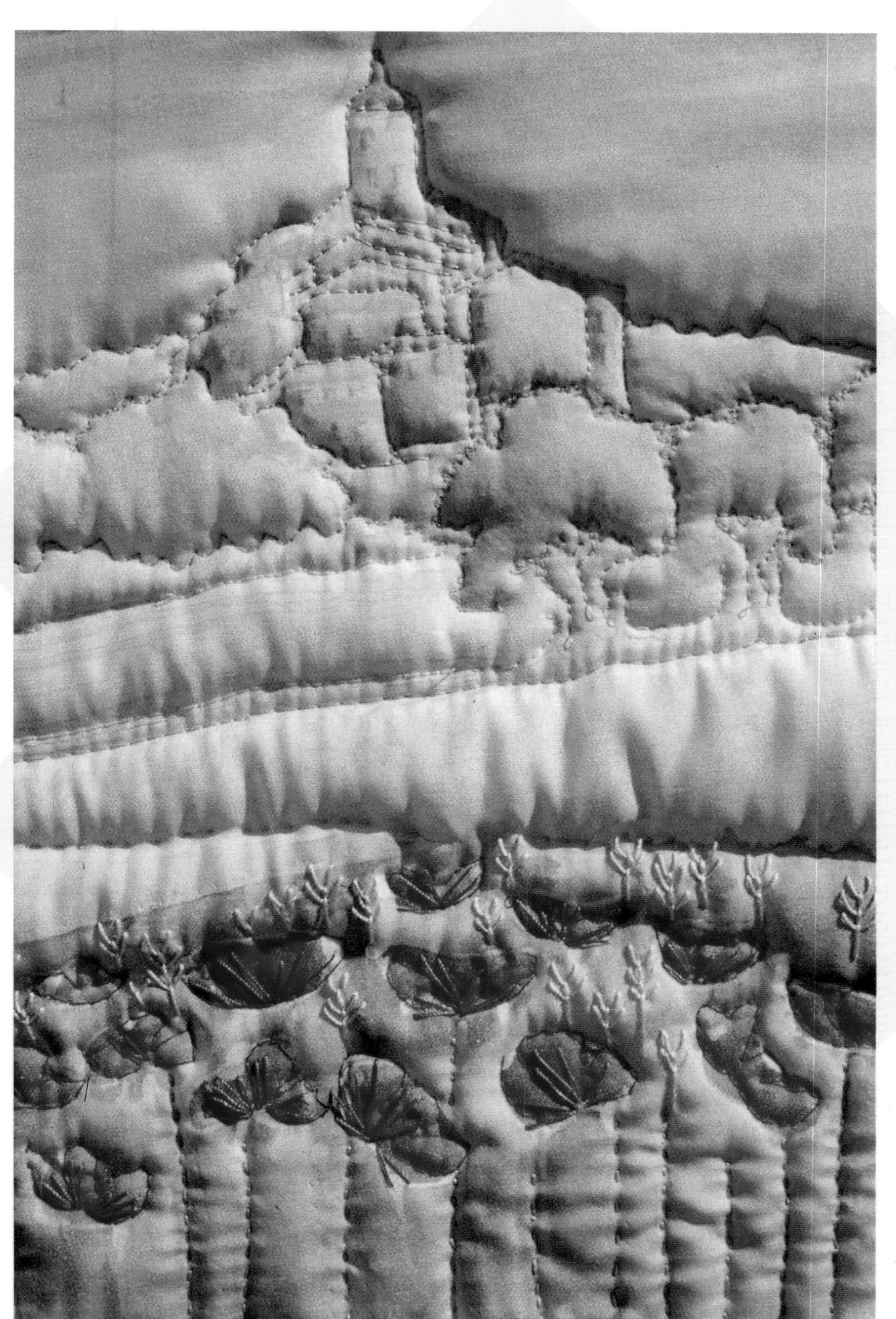

◀ **4**
Village in Provence. Fabric paint on silk, machine quilted and with some hand embroidery.

5
▲
Hand knitted fabric pieces applied and padded to create an effective stone wall.

6

Customer Lift. Padded figures in the 'lift' are set in a shallow quilted box.

7
▲
Jerusalem. Detail showing a knitted, padded head.

8 ▲ One World. Hanging at Guildford Cathedral by Margaret Rivers.
Detail to show how layers of fabric have been cut away.

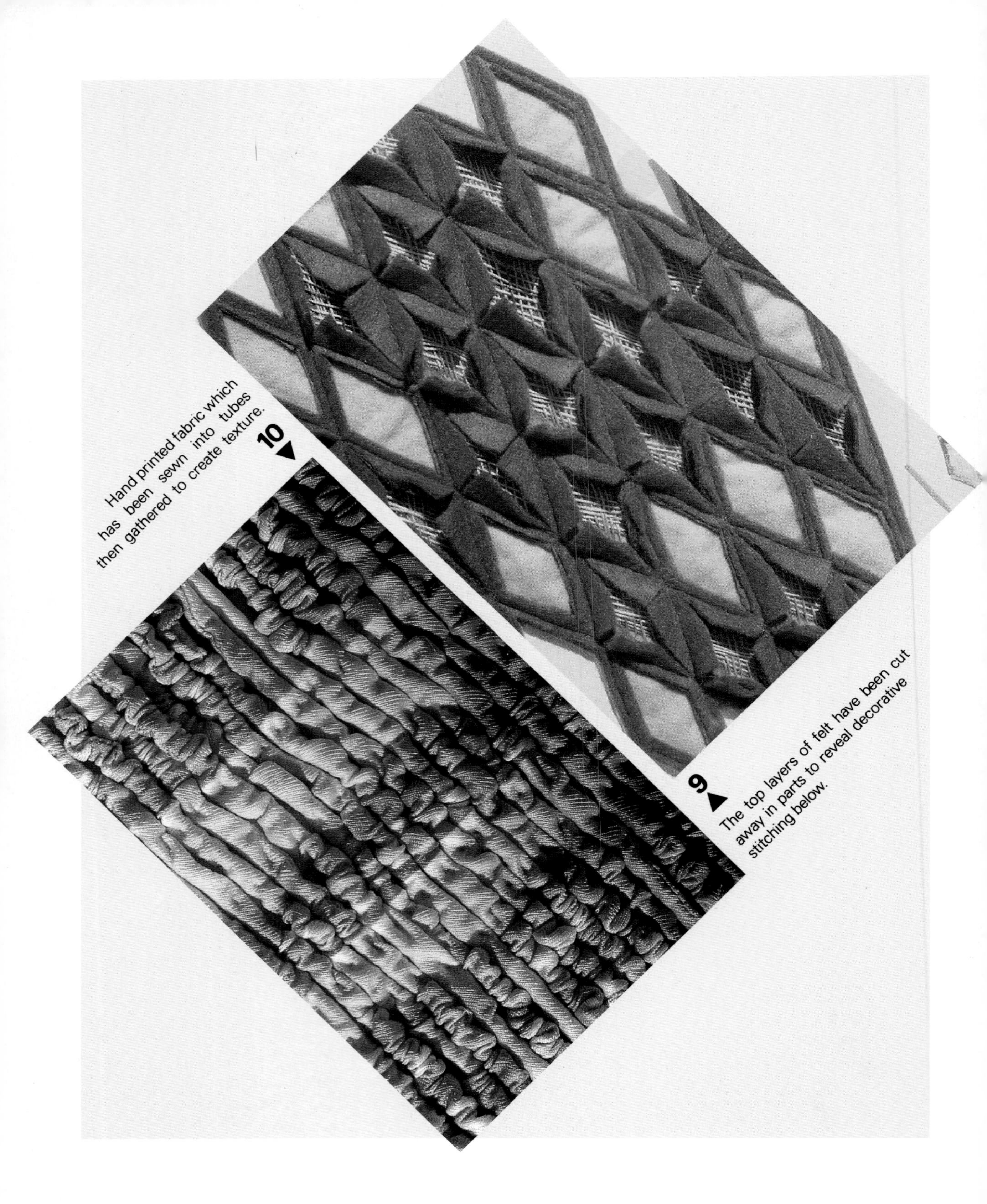

10 ▼ Hand printed fabric which has been sewn into tubes then gathered to create texture.

9 ▲ The top layers of felt have been cut away in parts to reveal decorative stitching below.

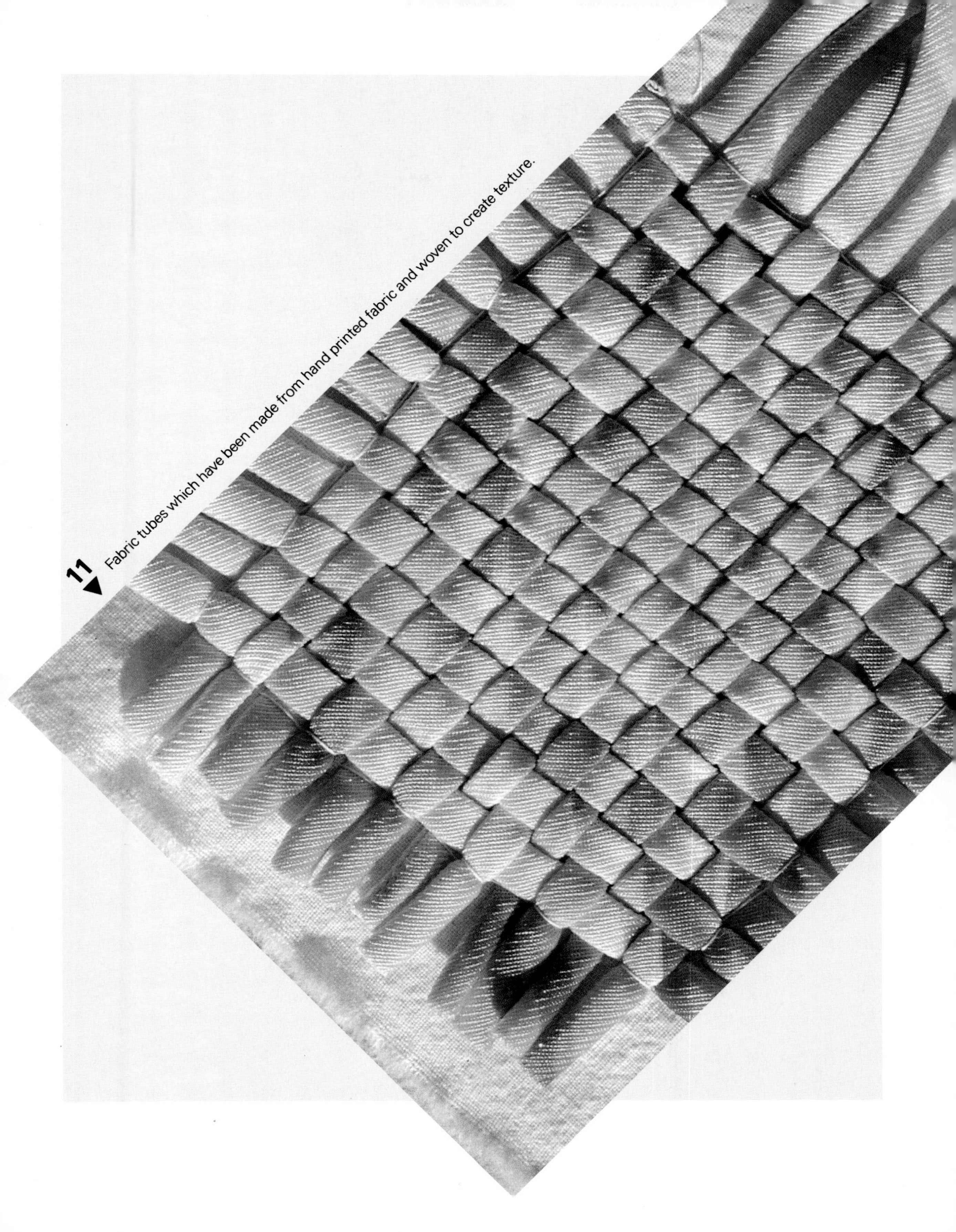

11 Fabric tubes which have been made from hand printed fabric and woven to create texture.

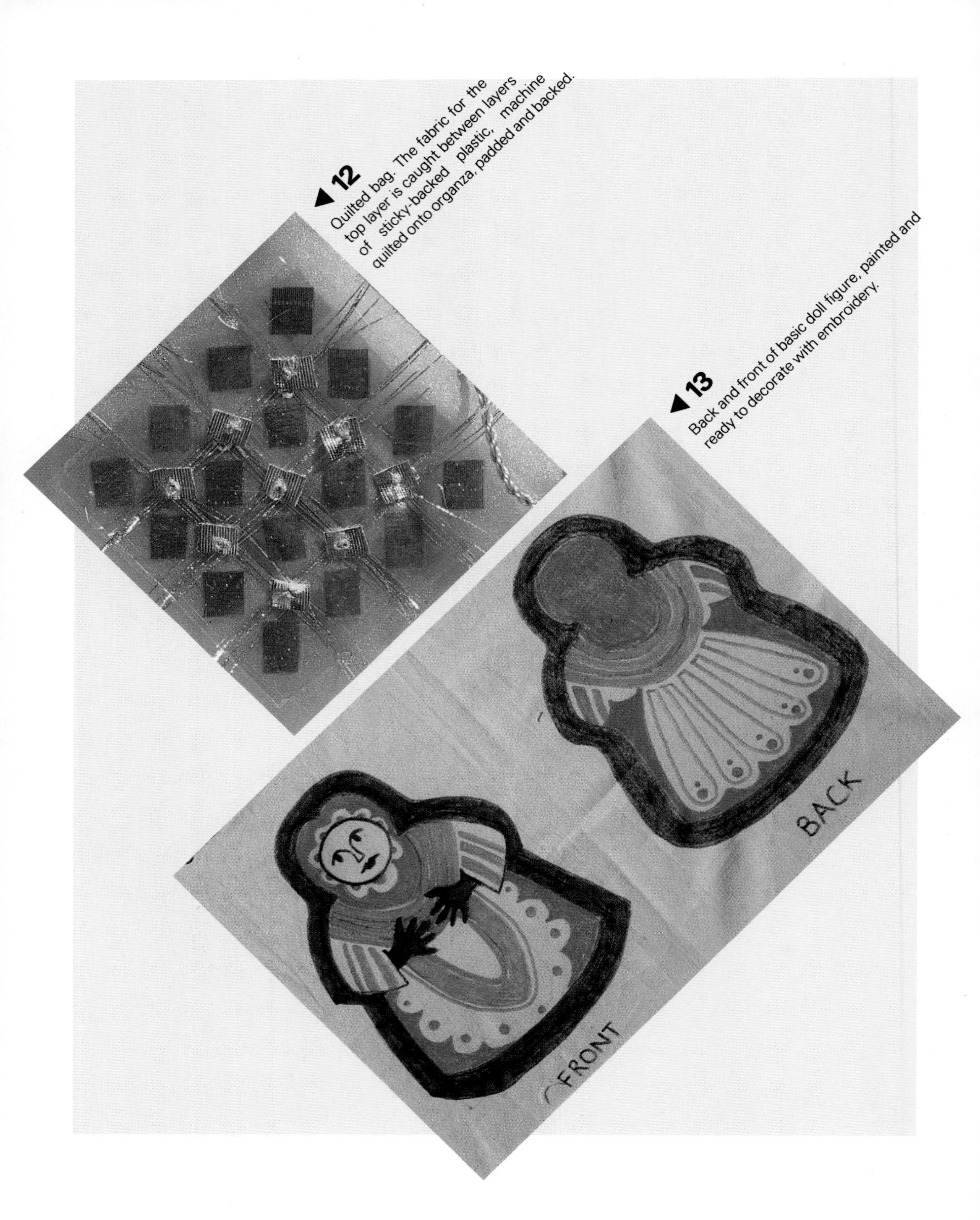

12 Quilted bag. The fabric for the top layer is caught between layers of sticky-backed plastic, machine quilted onto organza, padded and backed.

13 Back and front of basic doll figure, painted and ready to decorate with embroidery.

14
▲
The Vine, by Anne Wilson. All the fabrics have been hand painted and dyed. Bonded fabric leaves are stiffened with wire. Grapes of compressed paper are covered with nylon knit (tights). The stems are stockinette-covered rope.

15
▲

Stone. Stiffened muslin form with stretch velvet cover, decorated with needleweaving, spider's webs and applied machine embroidery.

16
▲

Totterdown, Bristol. Interlocking card house shapes were individually covered then sewn together and potato-printed with roofs and windows. Trees and steps were padded and machine quilted. Shrubs in the foreground are card shapes, covered and decorated with wrapped yarns.

17
▲
Lollipops. Card shapes covered with knitting and wrapped in plastic.

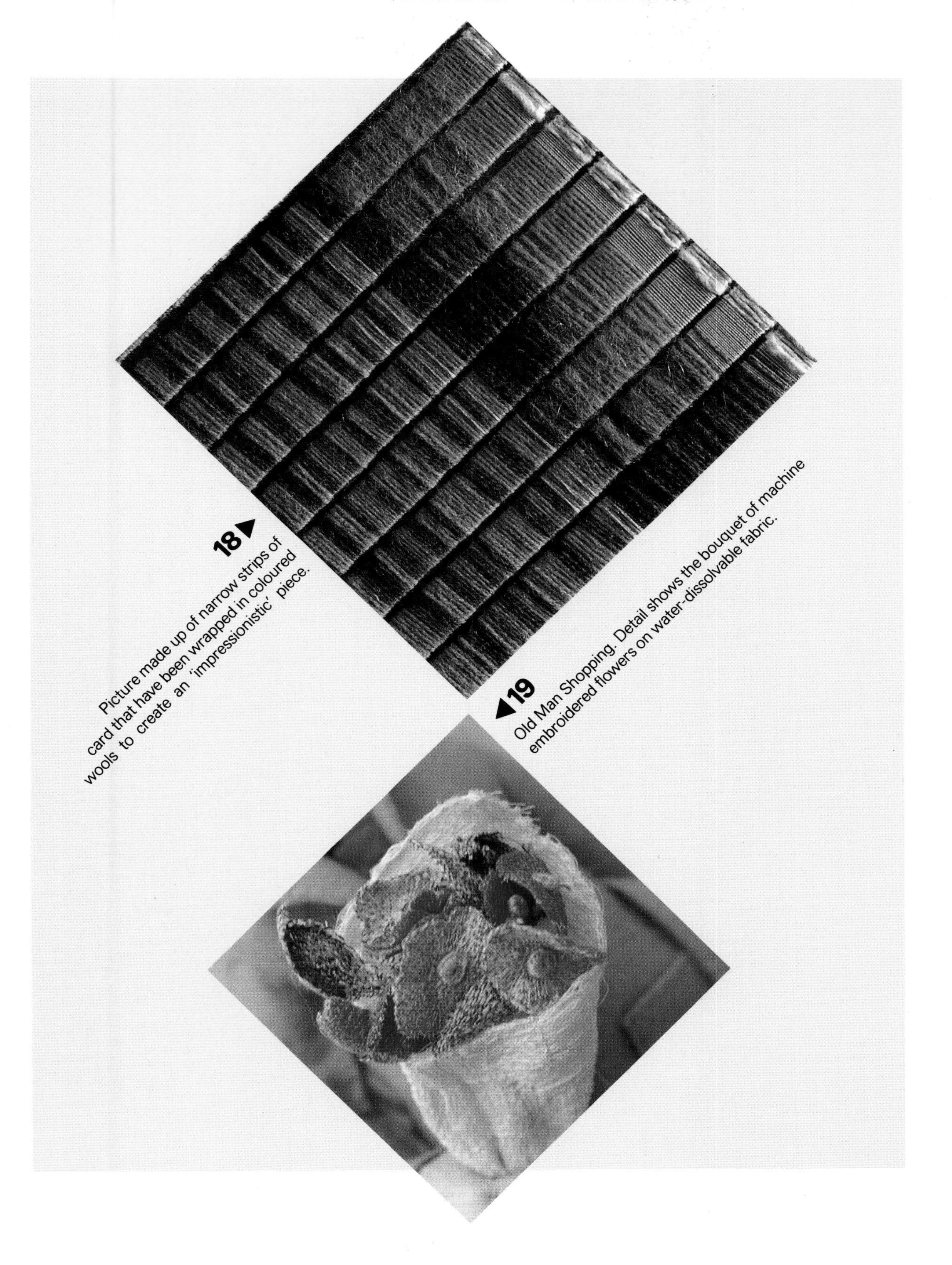

18▶
Picture made up of narrow strips of card that have been wrapped in coloured wools to create an 'impressionistic' piece.

◀19
Old Man Shopping. Detail shows the bouquet of machine embroidered flowers on water-dissolvable fabric.

20
▲
Surface raised with felt pieces and decorated with needleweaving.

41 Machine corded quilting.

42 Straight-line designs for machine corded quilting.

Method

Use woven fabrics to practise. Pin together so that the straight grain of the fabrics is running the same way. Allow the foot of the sewing machine to act as a width gauge, or use the markings on the base of the machine. Use a medium stitch length, with normal foot and machine settings.

Designs with straight lines

- Parallel lines can be stitched from one side to the other, either along the straight grain of the fabric, or on the cross.
- Use striped fabric, and follow the stripes of the fabric.
- The width between the lines of stitching might be unequal so that when the lines are quilted, some are more prominent than others.
- Instead of only two layers of fabric, several can be used. Then some layers can be cut away when the stitches have been worked. If some of the fabrics are woven and sewn carefully, it will also be possible to fray out some of the edges.
- The quilting yarn might be pulled up through holes cut in the top layer to form a texture.

Designs with straight lines and angles

You will need a sketchbook and pencil. These designs are so simple they can be drawn freehand and eventually copied with the machine straight onto the fabric. It is sometimes easier to design when the pattern is contained within a rectangle.

1 Draw several squares about 9 cm ($3\frac{1}{2}$ in.) square.

2 Start at one side of a square and draw a line part way across, then take it at an angle to the adjacent side. Draw a line parallel to the first, and continue drawing parallel lines on both sides of the first line to fill the square.

3 Fill in each square with a different pattern in a similar way.

Materials

The effect created by these patterns depends on the different materials that are used. Try some of the following:

- A very shiny fabric, where the light catches the patterns made by the stitches.
- A transparent top fabric. The quilting yarn can then be coloured or textured and will show through on the front.

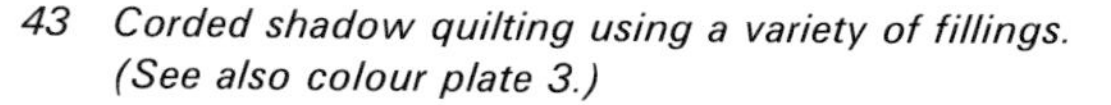
43 Corded shadow quilting using a variety of fillings. (See also colour plate 3.)

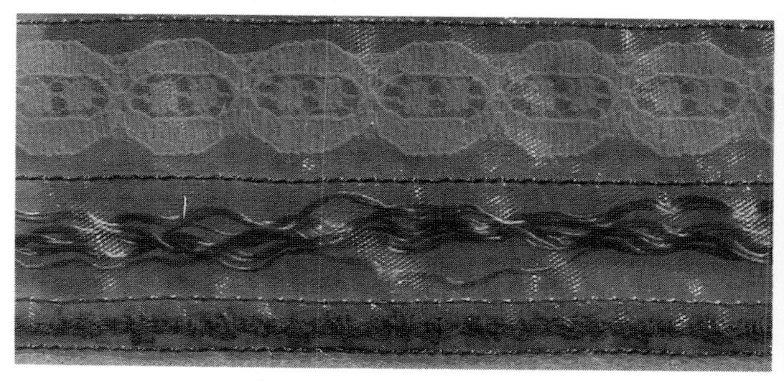

5

Experimenting with different fabrics and materials

Quilting appeals to a wide spectrum of people who are interested in the technique from completely different viewpoints. Patchwork enthusiasts are fascinated by the abstract patterns made by the arrangement of the patchwork pieces. For many of them, the quilting is merely a way of finishing and presenting. Others use the technique as a means of adding texture to a fabric picture or appliqué. Many people enjoy quilting garments and objects, using more functional fabrics with either traditional or modern patterns.

Some modern quilting looks quite different from traditional quilting not only because the patterns are arranged in a different way, but also because practitioners enjoy experimenting with a variety of fabrics and different materials, just for the sake of seeing what happens, in rather the same way as a scientist might work on an element to see how it reacts.

After having tried out some of the techniques of quilting on fabrics which are easy to manage, it is interesting to work with a variety of different materials to see what happens.The results can then be kept for reference so that when a larger piece of work is being considered, you will have some idea of how various materials react to being quilted.

44 Quilting on a commercially printed fabric.

TOP FABRICS

Shiny and metallic fabrics

The top fabric makes all the difference to the look of the finished work, and some fabrics are particularly beautiful when quilted, especially those which catch the light and throw up shadows made by the stitches. Look for silks and satins, particularly in plain light colours. Use a matching thread to show up the fabric to best advantage. Some silks and satins have a pattern woven into the surface, which might be incorporated into the design of the quilting pattern.

There are many very shiny and exotic fabrics with a bonded metallic surface, and wet-look fabrics like PVC, which quilt well. Do not use very small machine or hand stitches on these surfaces, which can tear easily. Occasionally a sewing machine will not sew evenly across a very shiny surface. Either sew between two sheets of tissue paper, or buy a non-stick surface to put on the base of the sewing foot.

Commercially printed fabrics

A large number of furnishing and dress fabrics are printed with patterns or motifs which might be suitable for quilting. Look for large, simple motifs or uncomplicated patterns. This method is very useful for soft furnishings, when making cushions, etc. Quilt along some of the lines of an all-over pattern, or quilt round some of the main motifs. Make sure the quilting is evenly distributed over the surface.

A motif can be applied to a plain background and quilted at the same time by pinning together the background, wadding and plain fabric with the patterned fabric on the top. Sew round the motif with straight stitch, then cut away the background and finish by sewing round the motif with close zigzag stitch. Work more quilting stitches on the background, following the shape of the motif.

Hand printed fabrics

Patterning by hand is a very satisfactory way of making a suitable and individual surface for quilting. Printing and painting can be done successfully on a small scale using a variety of paints and crayons which can be used in different ways to colour the surface of a fabric. It is a good idea to try out paint on small pieces of different suitable fabrics.

Follow the instructions on all paints and crayons very carefully as each is made for different fabrics. Make sure that fabric to be coloured is previously washed or soaked, if necessary, to get rid of any dressing. Press fabrics before painting or printing. Fabric prepared for printing can sometimes be obtained from a craft supplier. Leave a border of at least 10 cm (4 in.) round the edge.

Painting fabrics

Fabric paint is either opaque and can be used on light or dark fabrics, or transparent for use on fabrics lighter than itself. Opaque metallic paint is also available. Some paints are thick while others are thin and runny.

First try out the paints on small pieces of both natural and synthetic fabric. Hold the prepared fabric in a tambour ring, or stretched on a frame so that it is taut. This prevents paint seeping off the background surface back onto the fabric.

45 Quilted squares filled in with a fabric paint design.

46 Fabric which has been painted over areas of resist medium. (See colour plate 1.)

47 Quilting on a batik design.

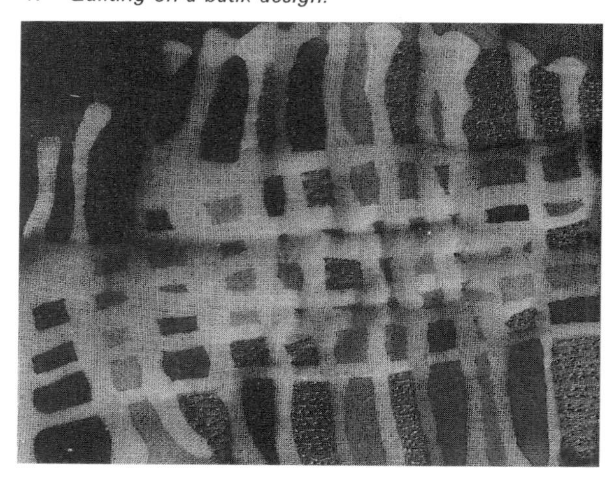

Try some of the following methods:

- Make multicoloured surfaces by dripping paint onto wet fabrics. Try the same colours on dry fabrics, perhaps using two colours together.
- Paint, dab and stipple on wet and dry surfaces to make marks and patterns. Use both thick and thin brushes.
- Make a patterned surface by quilting, then, with colour, fill in or mark each shape made by the stitches. Always allow the paint to dry before moving the frame.
- It is possible to buy a resist medium which can be painted between areas to stop paints running together. Batik wax is an alternative. Make sure the resist enters the fibres of the fabric and does

not just sit on the surface. Allow the resist to dry thoroughly before adding paint.

- Spray or splatter paint onto fabric. The frame should be stood vertically for spraying and the surrounding area protected with newspaper. Use either a spray diffuser or a loaded toothbrush. It is also possible to use a plant spray or an empty spray bottle. Try this out first on a spare scrap of fabric. Car sprays are very satisfactory, but it is important use them in a well-ventilated room.
- Spray through stencils. These can be cut and stuck onto fabric with double-sided tape. When the fabric is sprayed, the stencil resists the paint.

Printing on fabric

Print with the fabric pinned onto softboard over several sheets of newspaper or blotting paper. Any number of patterns can be printed very easily, using small printing blocks made from corks, potatoes, sponges, rubbers, etc. These can be used either to make a regular all-over pattern, or to create an area of informal pattern. Leaves and dried flowerheads with simple shapes also make satisfactory prints.

Transfer paints and crayons are for use on synthetic fabrics only, as follows:

1 Paint or crayon the design on flimsy paper (typing copy paper or greaseproof), then print by placing the design face down on the fabric and pressing with a hot iron. The ironing board needs to be well protected with newspaper. It is a good idea to test the paints and crayons on scraps of spare fabric before beginning.

2 Paint the paper with blocks, lines or patterns, then cut out shapes and arrange these on the fabric. Press. Another idea is to iron the papers over stencils or materials with holes like net curtaining, a doily, paper cutouts, etc.

3 It is possible to print with transfer paint onto paper using the same small printing blocks described above. The design is then ironed onto fabric. Remember that the design will be reversed.

48 India rubber prints

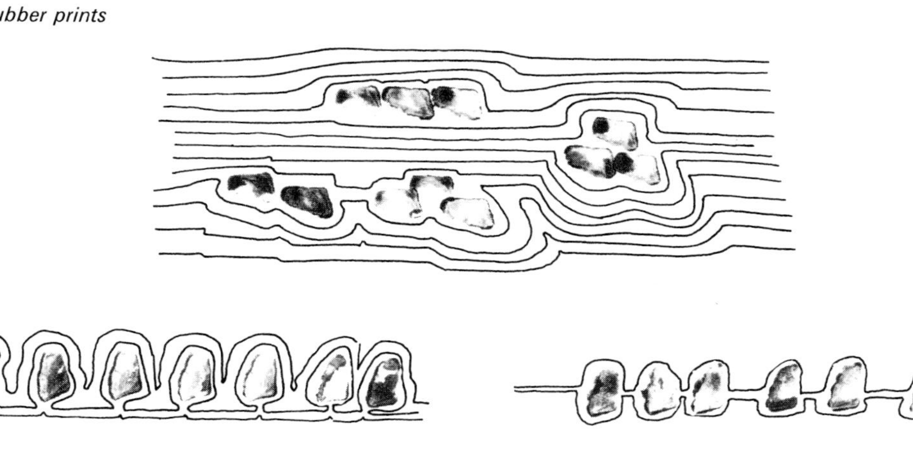

49 *Leaf print. Transfer paint on synthetic satin, hand quilted.*

50 *Flowerhead prints. Transfer paint on synthetic fabric, machine quilted background.*

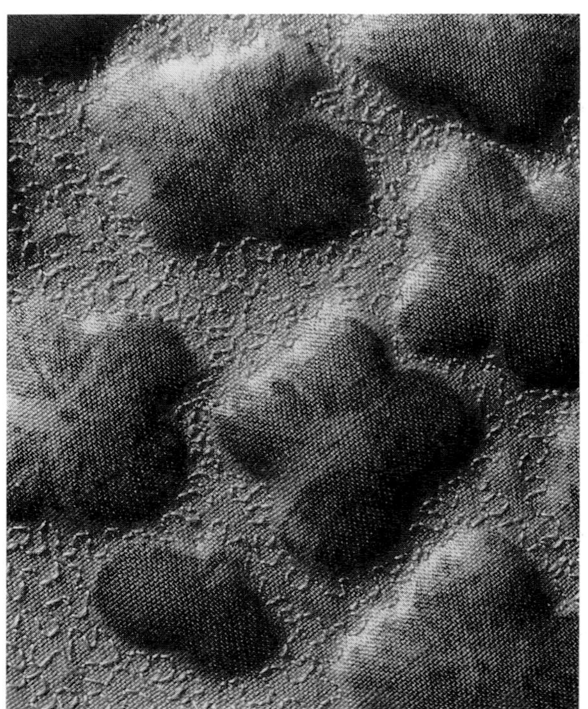

4 The crayons can also be used to take rubbings of fabrics, wood, embossed wallpaper and so on. Make a 'page' of texture which can be cut up and printed, or take rubbings of simple individual shapes like leaves or seedheads.

The pattern, motif or texture created by printing depends on what is required. What is printed might be a regular all-over pattern or a motif, a border pattern or a texture. Many people prefer to paint landscapes or figures or natural shapes like feathers, birds, fish and so on, which can then be further enhanced with quilting stitches. Whatever is printed should be a personal choice. However, the printed design and the quilting pattern should be considered together and should enhance one another.

The quilting stitches might be used in several ways:

- Following the line of the pattern, but *not* touching it, as it is a pity to print an interesting line then cover it with stitches. Other quilting lines might then follow the first line (Fig 49).
- The background can be flattened with a vermicelli-type pattern, throwing the subject into high relief (Fig. 50).
- Sometimes it might be most effective to have only one quilting line, giving an indented effect.
- Just one tie might be made every so often, giving a dimpled appearance. In any case make sure the quilting lines are not too close together, unless of course that is the effect you wish to create.

EXPERIMENTS WITH THE FILLING

The colour or pattern of the wadding or filling cannot usually be seen, but in shadow quilting, when using transparent and translucent fabrics, it is very important.

Organdie is a traditional material used in shadow quilting, where brightly coloured pieces of fabric and threads are caught between two layers of translucent fabric. There are also many other beautiful sheer fabrics, ranging from soft wispy chiffons to organzas shot with iridescent colours, and from silk to synthetics which can be used to good effect in the same sort of way.

Although the types of fabric available at any one time in department stores often depend on fashion, it is usually possible to find exciting fabrics in specialist theatrical suppliers which keep these fabrics at all times. Many shops cater for ethnic minorities where some lovely fabrics are sold. Some mail order firms stock sheer fabrics that are specially suitable for embroiderers. Another material which might be considered is plastic. At first sight it would seem rather an inferior material to mix with embroidery, but by using it carefully and with imagination, it can be transformed. It has the added advantage of being almost completely transparent. Each of these fabrics has an individual look so try some of the following combinations of fabrics and threads on a small scale.

Two sheer fabrics sandwiching fabric shapes (shadow quilting)

Cut out the shapes and tack onto one fabric. Tack the other fabric over. Stitch round the shapes either by machine or by hand. If the back does not show, the shapes can be stuck down with a very small amount of fabric glue or a small piece of double-sided bonding material. Traditionally, the middle fabric in shadow quilting is felt, which is very easy to handle. However, any fabric can be substituted and it is well worth exploring the possibilities of shiny, glittery fabrics or pieces of plain coloured fabrics. Handmade felts can be cut into shapes and caught between sheer fabrics and quilted, and synthetic wadding, which is normally white, can be dyed or coloured and used in the same way.

51 Two layers of machine stitched organdie. Trapunto quilting with yarns and wadding.

Found objects like coins, large sequins, lace motifs and so on can all be used as the filling in the sandwich.

Trapunto quilting with two sheer fabrics

Two fabrics can be handsewn or machined together, then stuffed with coloured wools or small scraps of fabric.

Sheer top fabric over an opaque fabric

A transparent fabric can be used to neutralize a bright patterned fabric. Sometimes a hand printed or commercial patterned fabric is too bright and gaudy and it can be redeemed by covering with a transparent fabric, then quilting through all the fabrics at the same time. The quilting stitches should enrich the pattern on the fabric. It is by trying all sorts of transparent and opaque fabrics together that you can see just what is possible. Sometimes the effect created is dull, but at other times it is surprisingly effective.

52 Fabric painting on synthetic satin with a layer of organdie laid over and hand quilted.

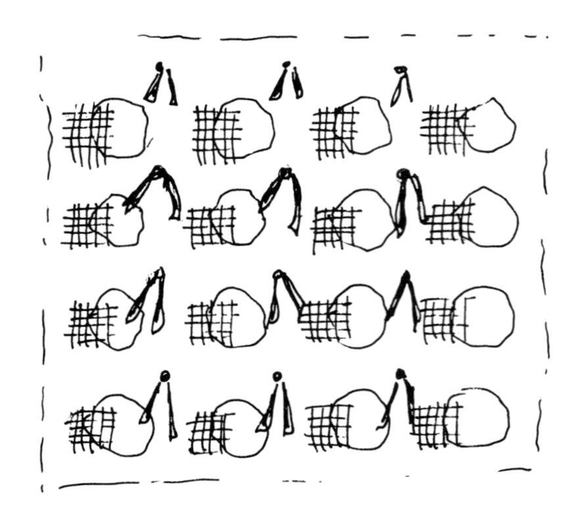

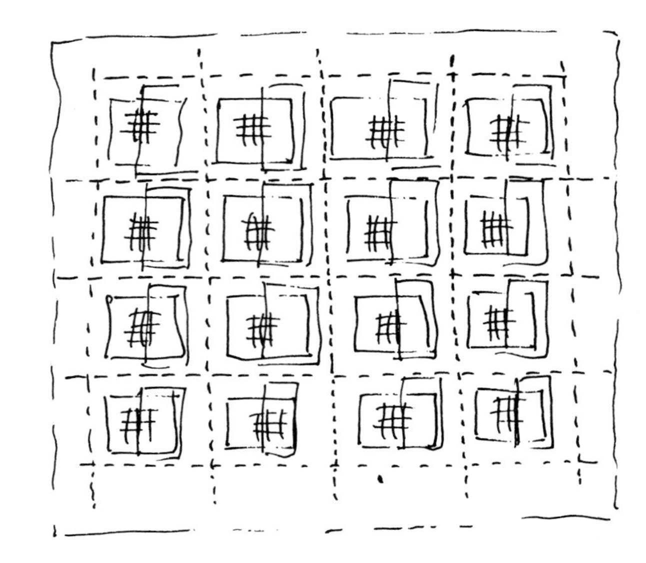

53 Pieces of thread and fabric caught between two layers of plastic.

Using plastic

Pieces of fabric and thread can be caught between two pieces of plastic. This exploits the look of fragility created by small pieces of wispy, exotic fabrics caught in a transparent medium. Static electricity makes it rather difficult to stop the bits from moving out of place but this can be overcome by using the transparent sticky-backed plastic sheet normally used for covering books. This is usually marked out in squares, so cut out a piece 4 cm by 4 cm ($1\frac{1}{2}$ in. by $1\frac{1}{2}$ in.) and attach it, sticky side up, to a plastic table top with a tiny piece of double-sided sticky tape. Arrange a pattern of threads or fabrics and threads on this using tweezers if necessary. Press down carefully. Cut a similar piece of plastic and press this to the first, sticky sides together.

It is difficult to do this on a large scale, as the plastic is apt to crease, so it is a good idea to design a small piece of work, or make several similar small pieces which can be put together to make a larger design.

Machine or hand stitches can be added using the plastic as a top fabric and sewing through wadding and a backing material. Stitches can also be worked just through the plastic. Because the materials are transparent, the ends of the working threads cannot be fastened off so they can be left to hang, adding to the insubstantial feeling of the piece.

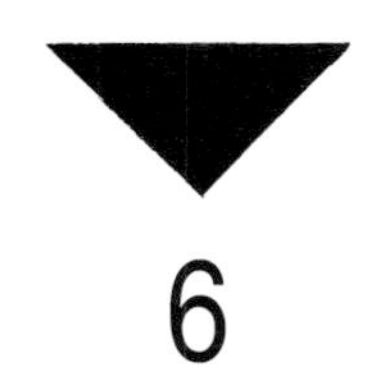

6

Patchwork and appliqué

The technique of sewing together small patches of fabric to form an all-over interlocking pattern reached its peak in America during the last century. Today, both in America and Europe, the craft is extremely popular and some of the quilts produced can only be described as works of abstract art.

These patchworks are made into quilts by adding a layer of wadding and a backing. The quilting stitches which hold the layers together either follow the patterns made by the arrangement of patches, or make a completely different but compatible pattern superimposed over the top. The craft of quiltmaking thrives because it combines art with function in a way many people find very satisfying.

It is beyond the scope of this book to go into methods of patchwork in detail, when there are so many excellent specialist books written on the subject, but anyone who is interested in quilting as a technique cannot fail to be impressed by the lovely quilts which have been produced, and a study of the stitch patterns used for the quilting shows that although they look extremely complicated, when analysed they are all based on geometric patterns like those described on pages 18–22.

Appliqué quilts evolved side by side with the geometric patchwork quilt. These were usually pictorial rather than geometric, and were made of very simple cutout fabric shapes assembled into a picture and sewn onto a square of plain fabric. These squares were then pieced together and quilted.

The technique of appliqué has evolved in several directions from picture quilts to single appliqué pictures and hangings, which might or might not be padded. Quilted landscapes are very easy to do and can be based on holiday sketches or snapshots.

54 *A patchwork of random dyed silk, hand quilted with metallic thread.* (Jenny Bullen)

55 Pattern for appliqué quilt. American, nineteenth century.

PROJECT: LANDSCAPE

Any appliqué picture can be padded but the result will be much more satisfactory if the quilted shapes are simple, and fairly large. Fiddly little pieces spoil the overall feeling of flowing, solid, rounded shapes which quilting conveys. Because of this it is necessary to simplify the initial design into areas of shape and colour.

A hilly landscape has been chosen as an example, because it already gives a quilted impression. The background (in this case the sky) can be completely flat, then as the applied shapes are built up and padded, they will take on a three-dimensional look.

1 Choose a suitable design, which might be a drawing or a photograph. A drawing is almost always easier because by drawing you automatically simplify what you see. However, it is a good idea to take photographs as back-up material.

56 Village in Provence. Padded appliqué with velvets, satins and printed cottons. (Compare the different techniques used for the scene in colour plate 4.)

2 Enlarge or reduce the design to the actual size you want to work. This is easiest to do on a photocopier, as the result is much more accurate. If you want a design bigger than the photocopier can manage, take a copy of the design and cut this up into a number of pieces which can then be photocopied individually. Do not cut up your original design.
3 Simplify the design by tracing off the main shapes and ignoring the detail. In this sort of work, simplification is of the essence. Everything we look at appears to have a shape, which might be an area of colour, of texture or of pattern. These shapes are most important in quilting, and they should not be too small because little pieces of fabric fray and disintegrate. Therefore, treat buildings as a single block, use only the outline shape of a tree or a copse of trees, and so on. This means that the initial observation of the shape must be particularly accurate. Large areas in the foreground of a picture might need to be broken up into smaller areas.
4 The patterns, colour and texture of the fabrics you choose should suggest the detail in the picture. For example, a flowery meadow might be a piece of fabric which is printed, painted or embroidered with flowers, but you could create just the same impact by using a fabric printed with splodges of colour or alternatively by using a very formal flower pattern. Even a striped or checked fabric in the right colours might suggest what you are trying to convey. In other words, you do not have to be too realistic to give the right impression. Look at a wide variety of fabrics to see which comes closest to what you want to convey. Sometimes a fabric will look much better if it is turned back to front or upside down, because of the way the light catches the weave. If you intend to colour, quilt or embroider any of the pieces, do this now. Mark out the area to be patterned with a fabric marker or tailor's chalk. Do *not* cut out at this stage.
5 Pin the fabrics onto a piece of soft board in the approximate order in which you intend to use them. Half close your eyes and stand away to get an idea of the tones (the lights and darks), and to see how the colours look balanced against each other. Make sure you choose the right tones for each part of the design and that none of the fabrics dominates in the wrong area. Dark and bright colours usually stand out more than pale, light colours. Patterned fabrics might look much darker or lighter at a distance than they do close up.

Working by hand

1 Choose a piece of background fabric and pin it onto a frame. Canvas stretchers are most convenient for this type of work. If the background fabric is too flimsy, back it with a piece of calico or cotton sheeting.
2 Cut out the individual pieces, using the pattern pieces traced from the design. Try to ensure that all the fabrics run the same way. Back those which do not with iron-on interfacing.
3 Lay the pieces on the background fabric. A landscape is particularly easy because you can start at the top and work down to the bottom, each piece overlapping the piece above. Some people prefer to leave a seam allowance to turn in the edge, but this is not absolutely necessary. A raw edge can also look attractive, and fabric can be fringed out to give a softer, three-dimensional look. Leave about 1 cm ($\frac{1}{2}$ in.) at the bottom of each piece for the overlap.
4 Tack and sew each piece down, using a small running stitch. When the top edge is sewn down, pad each shape with a little wadding, and tack down. The next piece then overlaps and is sewn in the same way, again adding wadding, but a little more this time, so that the padded areas become more quilted towards the bottom of the picture.

Using a sewing machine

If you are using a sewing machine, choose a paper-backed background fabric. You will not then need a frame.

Machine along the top edge of each pattern piece with a long straight stitch, then go over the stitch line with satin stitch. Pad out while working as for the hand method. The overall effect should be rounded and solid, and not be too much flattened by the stitching.

57 How to construct the appliqué picture.

Alternatives

- Make the whole picture as an appliqué, then lay the work over a layer of wadding and a backing, and quilt.
- Apply the pieces straight onto a fabric background tacked onto a layer of wadding and backing. Quilt through all layers at the same time.
- Paint the landscape onto a suitable fabric, then quilt.
- Use a plain coloured fabric like calico and stitch the picture in the same coloured thread to make a monotone.

7

Knitted fabrics

58 Pebbles by Iris Morris. Knitted fabrics (tights) used for trapunto quilting. The pebbles were later painted and decorated with hand embroidery.

Knitted fabric is a very exciting fabric on which to work, because it stretches, and so by padding out parts of the design using a trapunto quilting technique, it is possible to get a raised effect. The background fabric should be a firm woven fabric which will not stretch. There are a number of easily obtained stretch fabrics, for example jersey, nylon knit (tights) and stockinette. Many people are apt to forget that hand knitted fabrics are also very stretchy and by increasing and decreasing it is possible to create shapes which are even more three-dimensional.

59 Hand knitted fabric pieces, applied and padded. (See colour plate 5.)

PROJECT: QUILTED FACES

Many embroiderers shy away from the idea of depicting the human face, in spite of the fact that the results can be both amusing and interesting and something of a change from abstract patterns and natural objects. It is almost impossible to fail, and these sorts of faces can be tackled at all levels, both by beginners and experienced embroiderers, children and adults. It is difficult to see what is going to happen; it is almost as if a particular quilted character is waiting to be brought out of the materials.

Faces can be made either in relief, so that they stand away from the background, or they can be completely three-dimensional. It is important to remember that the more wadding used, the older, fatter and more characterful is the person who appears. If you want to depict a child or a young person, very little padding and very slight quilting is all that is necessary because children and young people have very smooth, flat faces. It is only with age and through the force of gravity that character and lines appear. Men, because they have much bigger noses and heavier bone structure, are easier to portray.

60 The Judge. Knitted nylon fabric, quilted and embroidered.

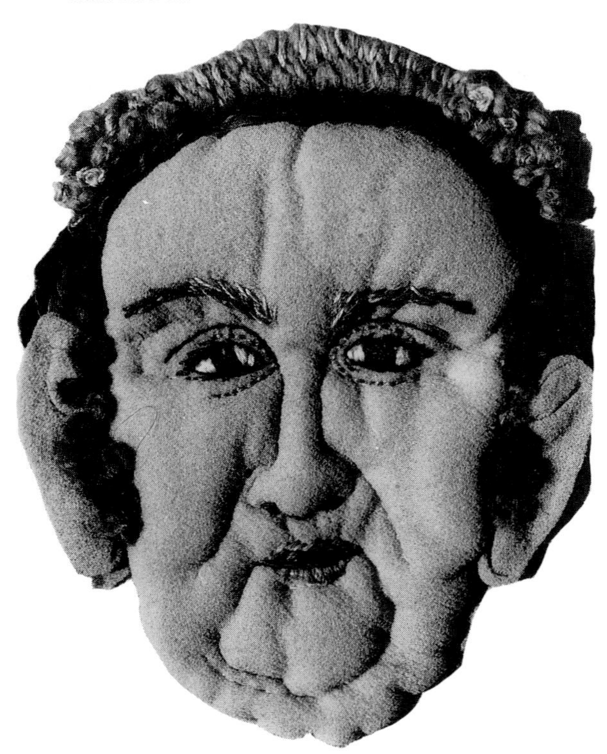

Before starting on this project, do some research by looking carefully at photographs and, more important, at the faces of people around you. Try to notice and record the proportions of the face. Examine the shape of a face when seen from the front. How low does the hair grow over the forehead? Notice how high the forehead seems on someone who is going bald. Notice too where the eyes are in relation to the top of the head and the chin, the position of the ears in relation to the eyes, nose and mouth, and the relationship of the forehead, cheeks and chin. People have quite big heads in comparison with the actual area of the features.

You can see your own face in the mirror, but it is fascinating to look at other people to see how such small differences in the proportion of the features can make such rich diversity. It seems that some people have missed beauty by only a millimetre, while others – with what seem like odd proportions when compared with the norm – are extremely attractive. Some people look beautiful in a photograph, yet quite plain in real life, and it is impossible to capture the true liveliness of some people on film. All faces have some interesting and pleasing features.

Collect different shaped mouths, noses and ears. See how much eyes can droop or turn up, while others are close together, or wide apart. Notice how small are the measurable differences, but what a difference they make.

Take photographs and make simple sketches or diagrams of friends and relations and look at photographs of people you would never dare approach personally. Padded faces are like caricatures; they are much more successful when based on reality.

61 *Background for Customer Lift. Figures padded over wadding, foam and card and sewn into an open, shallow, quilted box. (See colour plate 6.)*

Method

1 Use a woven fabric like calico or cotton as the background material, held taut in a tambour ring.
2 Referring always to your sketches, etc., cut a piece of wadding or foam in the shape of a face. Cut out another small piece of wadding and place in the nose position.
3 Cut out knitted fabric about 1 cm ($\frac{3}{8}$ in.) bigger than the wadding, place over the wadding, and pin lightly in place. Pin a piece of fabric in place for the neck but do not pad, or only slightly.
4 Quilt round the nose, from bridge to tip and round. Leave bridge unstitched. Sew with thread the same colour as the knitted fabric and use a back stitch. Pull the stitches tight, so they pull into the knitted face. If the nose seems rather small, you can add a little more wadding as you sew.
5 Turn the knitted fabric under the wadding and catch down firmly with a hem stitch. Leave a space for the ears.

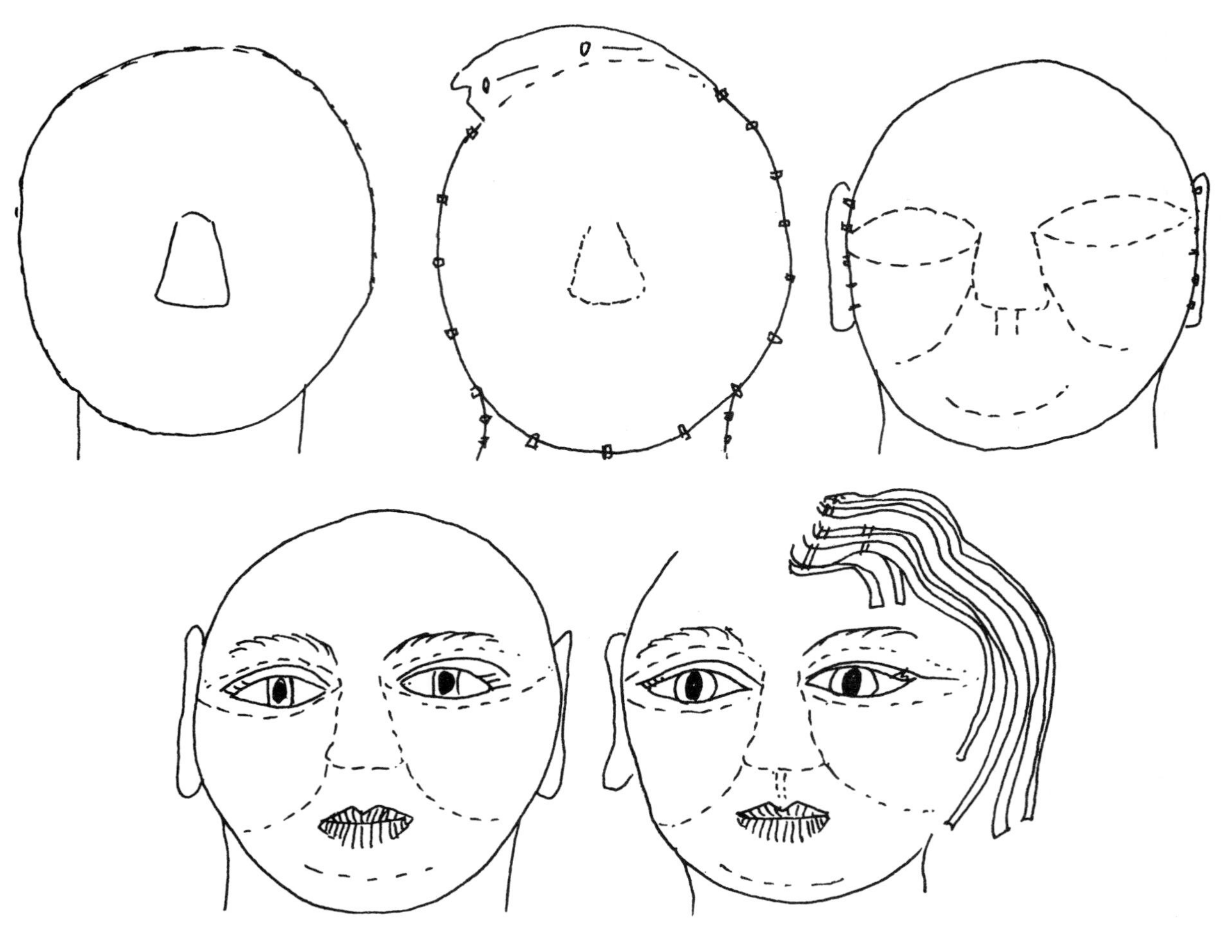

62 Constructing a fabric face.

6 Form eye sockets, using back stitch. Eye sockets should be big enough to accommodate the eyes comfortably.

7 To make the mouth and chin, back stitch the lines from nose to chin, and round the chin.

8 For the ears, fold a piece of fabric in half lengthways, and curve into an ear shape. Tuck under the face and catch down on the cheek side only and leave the other side to stick out.

9 Embroider a mouth, eyes, lashes, eyebrows, etc. Hair can be added by stitching or knotting thread onto the head. The materials used depend on the size of the face, which might be quite small or very big.

Faces can either be made in situ, or cut out and applied. They can be used for puppets as well as pictures, or just as a decoration.

Alternatives

As soon as you have made a basic face, it will become clear how you might experiment with other materials and ideas. For example, thick foam can be used, cutting the rounded shape of the forehead, the shape of the cheeks, and the eye sockets with a craft knife to give a more sculptured look. The eyeballs and nose could be cut as separate pieces, then all the pieces could be covered with fabric and built up to form the face. The eyelids and lips and ears could be made of folded fabric and added later.

Heads might be completely three-dimensional, from a simple stuffed sock toe, with features – the nose, eyebrows and mouth – pinched out and held in position with back stitch, to a sculptured head, formed by joining pieces shaped like the planes of the face and head.

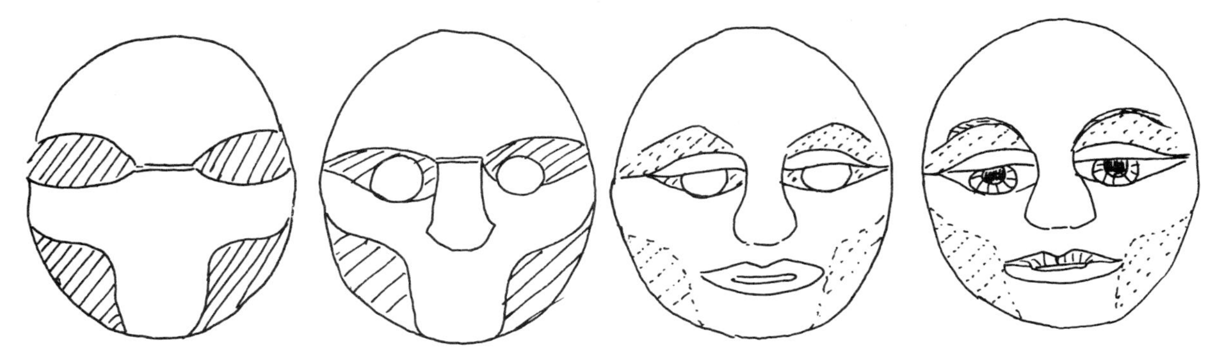

63 Each foam piece is covered individually in stockinette, then assembled.

64 Thick foam shapes are covered with stockinette and pinned to a background board so that stitches and further decoration can be added.

PROJECT: HAND KNITTED FACE

Use flesh coloured wool and size 3 mm (11) needles. Start at the top of the head and cast on 8 stitches. Increase 1 stitch at each end of every row for 3 rows, then at each end of every other row until there are 24 stitches. Continue straight down the forehead.

To make the nose, increase once on either side of the centre 3 stitches on both knit and purl rows for 4 rows, so that the nose is forced out. Alternatively you can put 3 stitches on a safety pin, continuing to knit straight down the cheeks, one at a time.

Increase the stitches on the pin to make a triangle shape (about 12 or 14 stitches over 12 rows). At the tip of the nose, decrease rapidly by knitting 2 stitches together twice at each side of the centre 3 stitches, then 3 stitches together on the next row on either side of the centre stitch to get back to the same number of stitches as at the forehead.

Knit 4 rows for a top lip.

Cast off 8 stitches in the middle to form the mouth, then on the next row make 12 stitches for the bottom lip. (This makes the bottom lip curl over in a most realistic manner and, as you knit, you wonder if you are taking part in a more divine activity than you previously realized!)

To form the chin, knit 2 together at the edge of the mouth on both sides and thereafter decrease in the same place on every knit row until the chin is formed. Knit the rest of the stitches in rib (K1, P1) to form a neck.

You can then go on to pick up the stitches on the bottom lip, and knit the inside of the mouth, sewing onto the top lip. And teeth –these might be beads or a pleated strip of cloth.

Embroider the eyes and eyebrows. Add hair.

Quilt this form over wadding onto a firm background, padding the nose, etc. as before.

There are any number of variations which might be employed. The face can obviously be knitted either on a much smaller or a much bigger scale. The eyes might be formed as slits. A bead could be sewn behind to make a more realistic eye. The mouth might be left open or closed. The ears might be knitted with the face. The head might be made three-dimensional by knitting a shape for the back of the head and joining the two together. The effects are all made by increasing, decreasing, casting on and off, and it is well worth experimenting with these techniques.

65 Jerusalem. Knitted and padded heads applied to a background of canvas embroidery.

8

Flat and gathered quilting

Flat quilting is used for sewing together two layers of fabric with a pattern of stitches, and is similar to wadded quilting, without the wadding. In clothes and furnishings the method might be used to strengthen the top fabric, either because it is too flimsy or worn or to add some weight or extra warmth.

Flat quilting can be done by hand, generally in back stitch, or by machine. The lines of stitches give the fabric a slightly indented appearance, as well as holding the two fabrics securely together. Flat quilting is sometimes used with trapunto quilting to anchor the areas of fabric which are not quilted.

MATERIALS

To try this technique, choose a top fabric which is easy to use. The fabrics used to practise wadded, corded and trapunto quilting are all suitable.

BY HAND

Pin and tack the fabrics together. Use back stitch or chain stitch, or any stitch which makes a definite line. Choose a simple all-over design, for example a grid of lines, a series of interlocking shapes like circles or diamonds, or a vermicelli pattern. Work from the centre to the sides of the design.

ON THE SEWING MACHINE

Try out free machine embroidery patterns with this technique, using a machine embroidery ring to hold the two fabrics in place. Experiment with several different types of top fabric and compare the effects achieved. For example:

- Use shiny fabrics like satins and plastic-coated gold fabrics. Work with a gold machine thread on the top of the machine.
- Thick felt produces a very indented 'carved' appearance. Handmade felt is not difficult to make, and the results are very much softer, deeper and more interesting than commercial felts. Terylene wadding can be dyed or sprayed and used as a top fabric, giving much the same look.
- Suede and soft leather can be enhanced with a pattern of stitches.
- Vary the top thread on the machine, use variegated thread, or use a metallic thread. Thicker top stitching threads are readily available. Loosen the top tension very slightly so that the stitches stand out. Use either straight or zigzag stitch. Narrow satin stitch gives a good line.

Many of these decorative techniques can be used for garments and furnishings, as well as experimentally.

VARIATIONS

In traditional flat quilting, two layers of fabric are used for practical reasons – strength and warmth – but if the technique is only decorative, some very interesting and exciting results can be achieved not only by cutting away some areas in the top fabric after the stitching has been done, to reveal the fabric underneath, but also by using several layers of fabric instead of only two.

To try this out, pin together three layers of plain woven cotton in different colours. With the sewing machine, and using straight stitch or satin stitch, sew through all three layers, stitching from one side of the fabric to the other, then from top to bottom, to make a grid pattern. Keep the lines of the design at least 3 cm ($1\frac{1}{4}$ in.) apart. With sharp scissors, cut away some of the areas of the top fabric between the stitches to reveal the layer underneath, or cut through two layers to show the bottom fabric. Leave some areas uncut.

This technique produces what looks like a checked fabric, which is quite padded and, if you have used satin stitch, will also be quite strong. Experiment with various combinations of fabric, and with different layers, as many as the machine will permit.

66 Layers of fabric machined and cut away.

67 Cutting away layers to create different effects.
(a) Using several layers and a variety of fabrics.
(b) Silk over net to create a lace effect.
(c) Cutting away fabric to a bottom layer of canvas on which stitches are worked.

a)

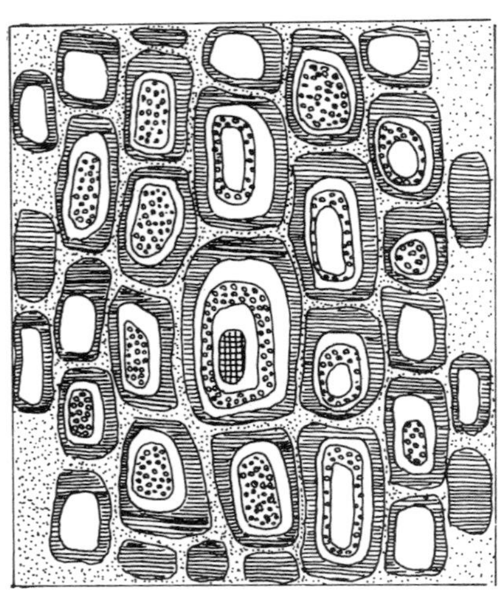

b)

c)

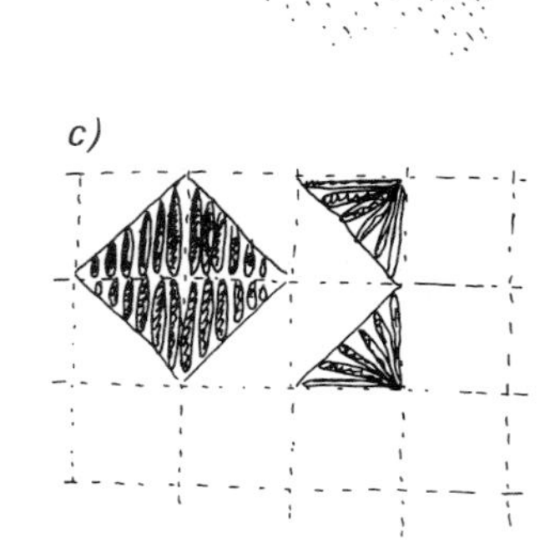

It soon becomes obvious that fabrics need to be chosen which look attractive together, so try out a variety of different types of fabric. For example:

- Incorporate a layer or two of sheer fabric.
- Use all sheer fabrics.
- Use a top layer of silk fabric with a bottom layer of net, so that when parts of the top layer are cut away the design seems to be floating on the net like Carrickmacross lace.
- Use colour co-ordinated plain and small-patterned fabrics.
- Use plastic as the bottom fabric.
- Use canvas as the bottom fabric. Sew the fabrics together, following the lines on the canvas. When the top fabric is cut away, the canvas is revealed and stitches can be worked on it. This method looks particularly attractive if the top layer is handmade felt or a rich fabric like velvet.
- Use several layers of felt in tones of one colour.

Try out ideas so that you can see what is going to happen and how the fabrics look together. You will find that the more layers of fabric used, the wider apart should be the lines of stitching. Otherwise there will not be enough room to cut and sew.

The number of layers used depends on the capacity of the sewing machine. Some machines will sew through as many as twenty layers of fine fabric like muslin or tarlatan.

SLASHING AND BRUSHING

Two, three or four layers of only one colour give a 'carved' effect, and by using a sharp craft knife, cuts can be made at an angle into the layers of fabric, or V-shaped slashes can be made rather than cutting the fabric away completely.

When layers of fabric are cut at an angle, they are apt to fray out, unless non-fray fabrics are used. However, if the fabrics are stiffened first (see pages 74–6), fraying can be prevented. On the other hand, the cut fabrics can be brushed to fray or fluff out if that is what you want to do.

CUTTING AND FOLDING

Other raised surfaces can be made by careful cutting and folding of the top layer or the top two layers of fabric. Again, the final result will depend on the types of fabric used.

Closely woven fine fabrics, like organzas and chiffons, and natural soft fine fabrics like muslin and cotton, which will gather and fold well but do not

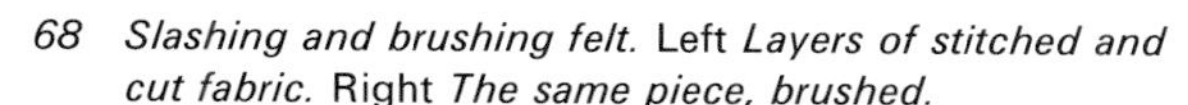

68 *Slashing and brushing felt.* Left *Layers of stitched and cut fabric.* Right *The same piece, brushed.*

69 Layers of cut and brushed cotton fabrics.

70 Jungle by Alison Sutton. Made for her daughters to use, with pockets, zips and openings to hold bits and pieces.

fray easily, are all suitable. There are many synthetic fine knitted fabrics, some coated with metallic plastic, which stretch easily and will not fray. Felts can be used and fabrics which fray easily can be stiffened.

When carrying out any of the following ideas, it is important that woven fabrics which are likely to be pulled out of place should be cut on the cross, and laid onto a base fabric which is cut straight. Do not be afraid to try out unusual fabrics and materials like handmade felt, plastics and paper.

1 Cut along only one side of some areas to make pockets. If the fabric is sheer, these can then be stuffed with contrasting fabrics or threads, some of which can be left hanging out. This method could also be used in a pictorial way by using each pocket to hold a three-dimensional figure.

2 Cut along three sides of an area and fold back the flap. Catch down.

3 Cut across on the diagonal or both diagonals, or cut a vertical or vertical and horizontal slits and fold or pull back the fabric. Either leave to stand free or catch down. The area revealed can then be decorated with stitches or beads or it can be painted. If the area revealed is big enough, another area can be machined and cut away to show a further layer, and so on. Slits can be cut in the bottom layer and a strip of fabric or ribbon pulled up in loops.

To start with, all these methods are very much more successful if the basic design is simple. Design can be based on the grid patterns which were explored in the chapter on wadded quilting, or on very simple patterns of geometric shapes, rectangles, triangles and diamonds or circles.

4 Machine parallel lines of stitches then cut between the lines of stitches. Machine across at right angles, pushing the cut fabrics to one side. Machine in the opposite direction, pushing the cut fabrics the other way and so on over the whole area. This is very successful with felt, coloured interfacing or fine suede, as both sides of the fabric are the

71 Cutting and folding.

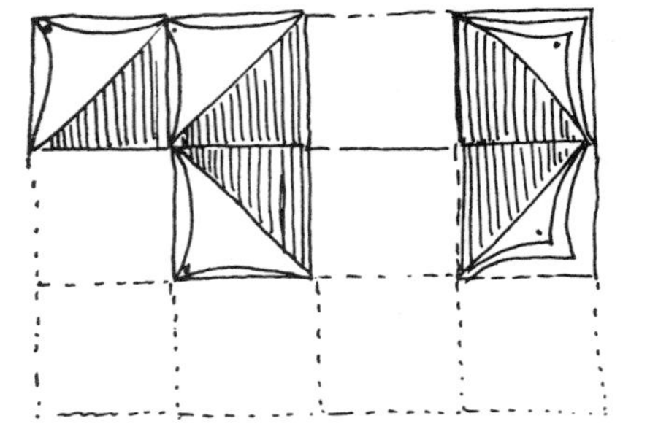

same and all have a slight stretch. If woven fabric is used, machine on the cross, with the bottom layer on the straight. By experimenting with a variety of fabrics and combinations of fabrics, paper and plastics, this simple technique can give some stunning results.

MAKING TEXTURE: GATHERED QUILTING

Areas of fabric can be gathered and applied to a background, or stuffed and applied to a background to make raised textured surfaces and patterns. Very effective, three-dimensional fabric knobs can be made in any size ranging from small round forms using transparent fabrics padded with coloured or glittery fabrics to large stockinette forms which might be used for puppet heads.

73 Machining across parallel lines of cut felt in different directions.

72 Layers of felt with the top layer cut away to reveal stitches. (See colour plate 9.)

Cut a round piece of fabric. Starting with a knot, make a circle of running stitches. Pull these up tight to enclose some sort of filling. Try out fabrics like silk filled with wadding, organza filled with coloured yarns or snippets of shiny fabric. Knitted fabric like nylon (tights) will stretch to accommodate a large amount of wadding. Plastic bubble packing might also be used to make an area of texture. Fill the bubbles from the back and stop the filling from falling out with sticky-backed plastic. Individual knobs can be applied to a background or a larger piece of fabric can be textured with padded knobs.

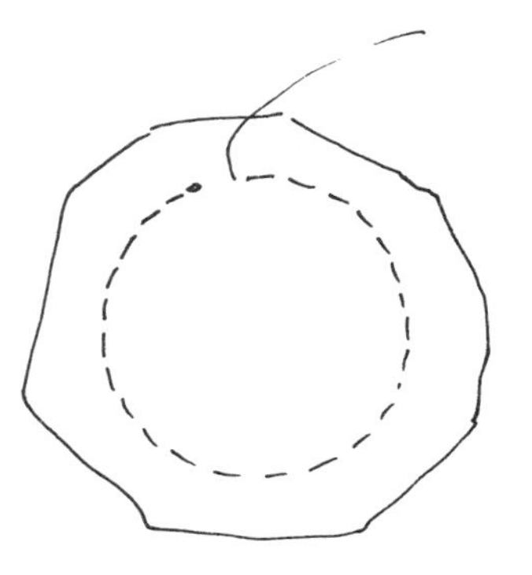

74 Making a fabric knob.

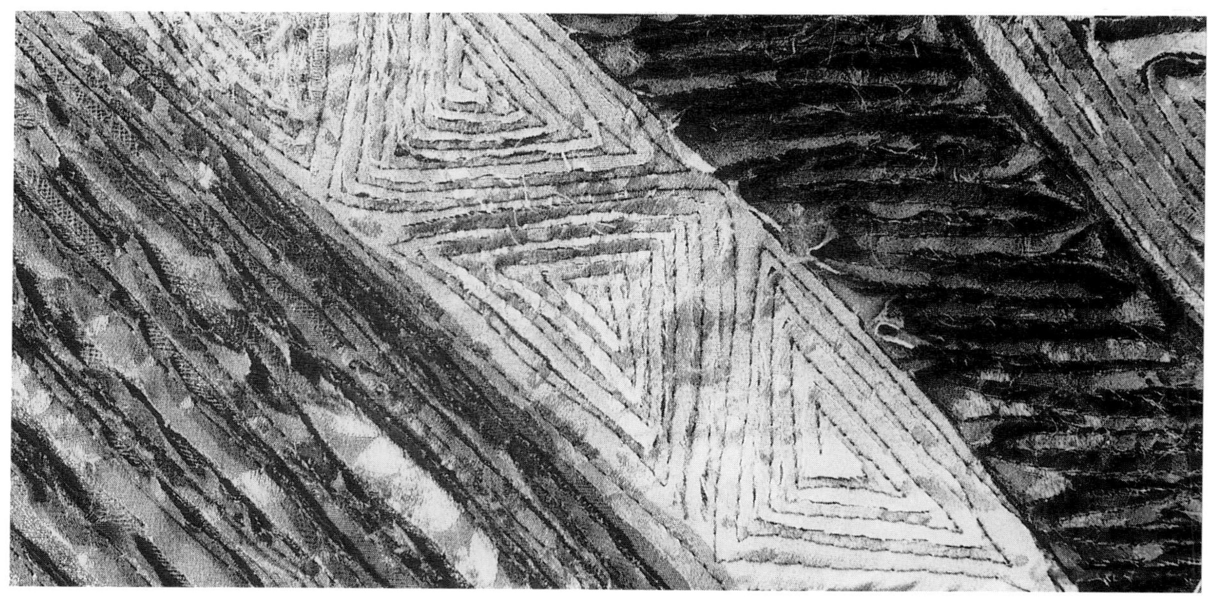

75 Layers of slashed silk.

76 Padded fabric knobs: part of a flowerhead.

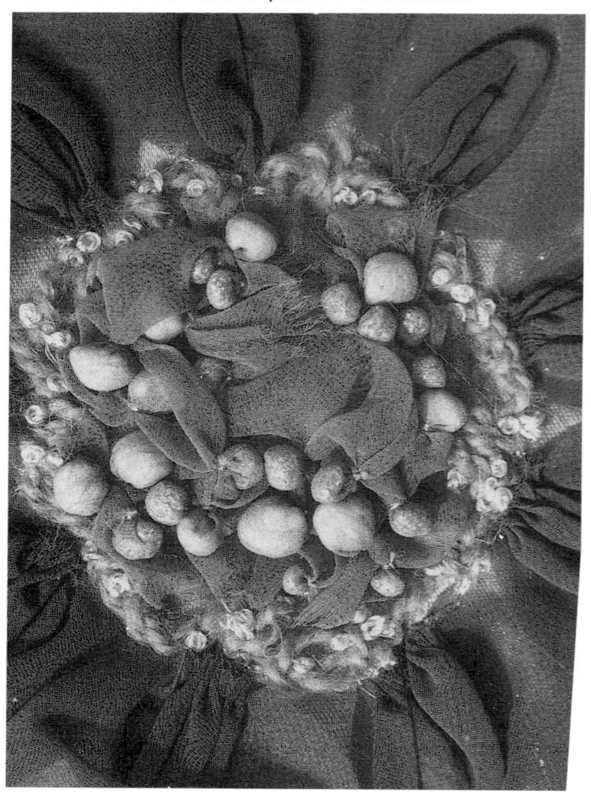

Gathered circles

Cut a circle of cloth about twice the size of the area which is to be covered. Turn in the edge with running stitch. Do not finish off at this point, but gently gather the thread so that the fabric bags. Apply to the background with slip stitch. Catch the fabric down at intervals with stab stitch, to give a texture. This method looks particularly good with shiny fabrics like satin, and soft fabrics like velvet.

Suffolk puffs

Cut circles of fabric, using a template if you want them all the same size. Gather as above, only this time the fabric is gathered tightly so that there is only a small hole in the middle. Finish off securely. These puffs are used with the hole facing outwards. Sew onto a contrasting background as decoration, or join together to make an all-over pattern. Traditionally the puffs are made with fabrics like

77 Gathered circles.

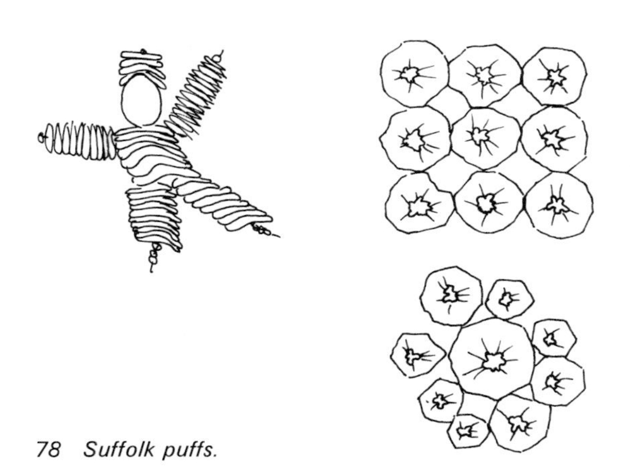

78 Suffolk puffs.

printed cotton, but it is interesting to experiment with other fabrics. The puffs might also be padded out with a contrasting fabric or thread to make them more three-dimensional. A number of puffs can be strung together to make a child's toy.

Gathering an area

Fabric can be gathered in lines with running stitch to make ridges, or with herringbone stitch to create a patterned texture. Mark out the position of the stitches on the back of the fabric before beginning, and gather as the work progresses.

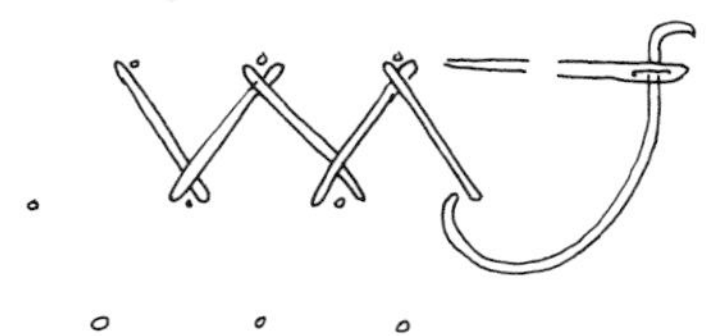

79 Herringbone stitch.

80 A variety of textures in different fabrics.

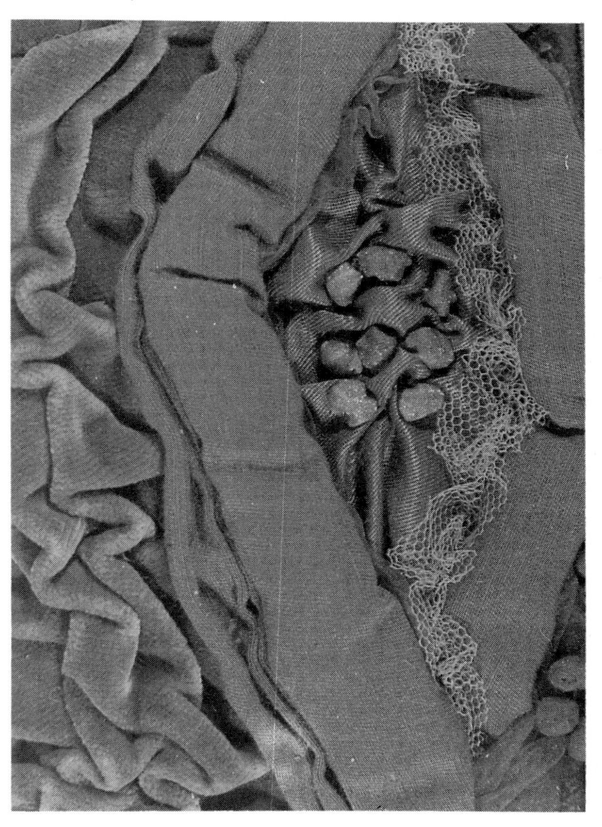

9

Quilting into three dimensions

All types of quilting give a raised texture, but shape can be converted into form by sewing two exactly similar shapes together and padding out the result to make a three-dimensional form. Three-dimensional lines can be created with stuffed fabric tubes.

Forms can be used in different ways:

- They can simply be attached to the background by sewing, or they can be tucked into pockets or slits.
- Several similar forms can be joined together to make a high relief pattern.
- Forms of all types can be used together to make a high relief picture.

81 Patterns that are suitable for three-dimensional forms.

MAKING FORMS

It is easy to make two-sided forms provided these are simple. It is essential that complicated arrangements are broken down into a range of simple shapes and lines which can then be constructed separately and put together again. For example, a flower might be made by first constructing all the petal shapes, then putting them together in the right order.

There are several ways of constructing simple forms, and the method chosen depends on the size, whether there are sharp corners, whether shapes have been printed or painted first and need to be easily visible, and so on.

Smaller shapes which might be difficult to turn inside out can be made using either the wadded method or the trapunto method (see below), but in any case the shapes should be of reasonable size or they will disintegrate. Experiment first to see which method works best.

82 Construction of a flower form.

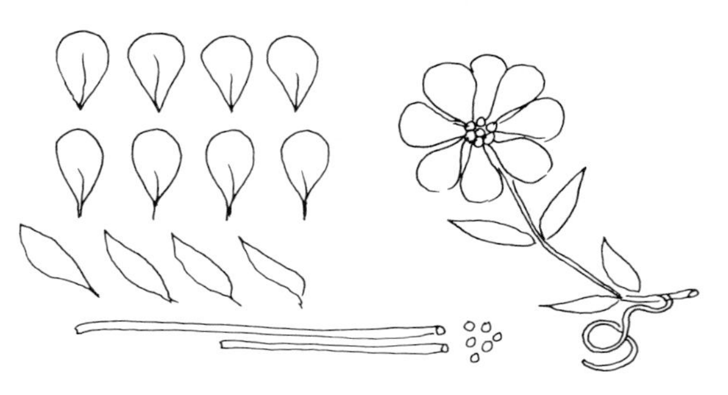

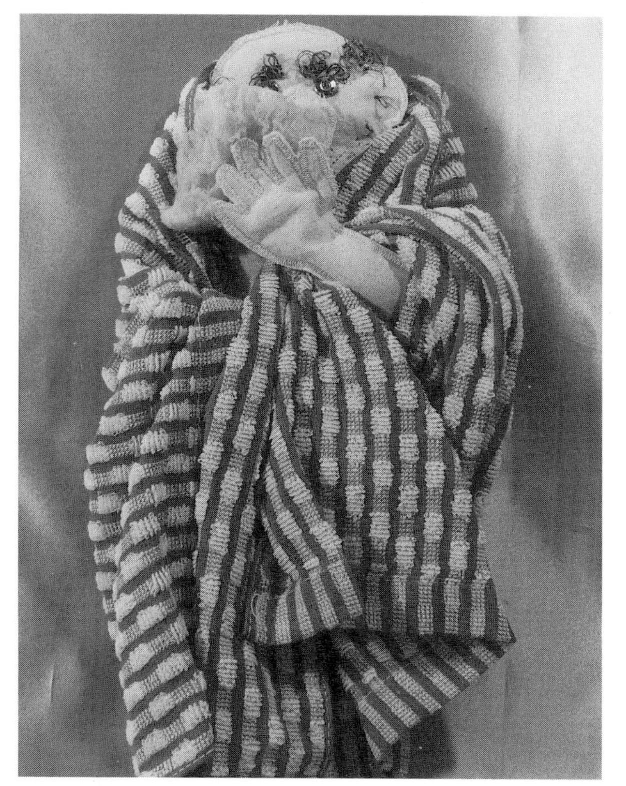
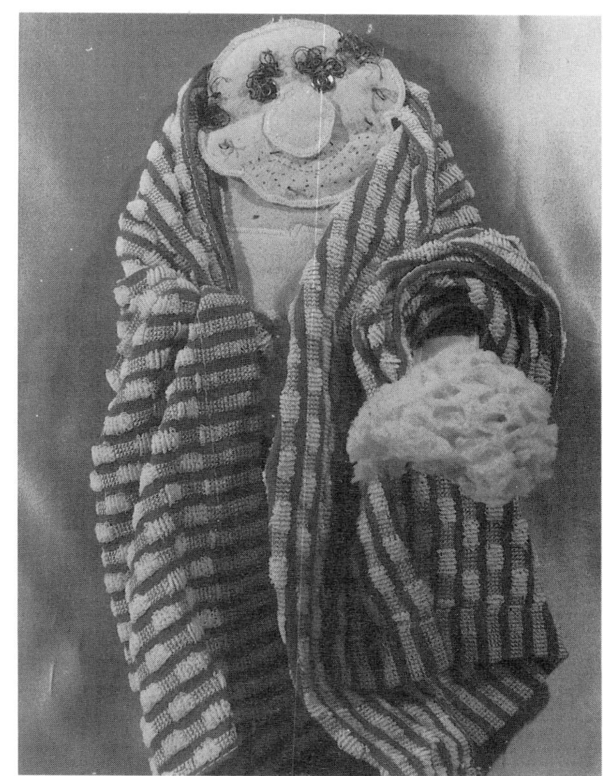

82 Flat Mates by Jennifer Westward. Flat figure made in separate pieces, then assembled and decorated. Press studs on the palms, eyes, etc. ensure that forms can be moved into different positions.

Wadded method

1 Sandwich a layer of wadding between two fabrics.
2 Mark out the shape on the surface and machine around it with straight stitch.
3 Cut out the shape and neaten the edge with satin stitch.
4 More stitch lines can be added either by hand or machine to quilt and decorate the surface.

Trapunto method

1 Using two layers of fabric securely pinned together or held in a frame, mark out the shape on the surface.
2 Machine round each shape with open zigzag stitch. Cut out the shape.
3 Make a hole or slit in the back, and pad the shape with wadding. Sew up the hole.
4 Finish with satin stitch round the edge.
This method gives the chance of variety in that some shapes might be really well padded while others are almost flat.

84 Chickens. Forms are hand painted and machine stitched, turned and stuffed.

Larger shapes

1 Use two layers of fabric, right sides facing. Mark out the shape and machine round, leaving a 2-3 cm ($\frac{3}{4}$-1$\frac{1}{4}$ in.) gap for stuffing.
2 Cut out the shape, leaving a seam allowance of 1 cm ($\frac{3}{8}$ in.).
3 To give smooth curves, cut through the seam allowance just to the machine line at intervals along concave curves. Cut away triangles of fabric on convex curves. Trim sharp corners.
4 Turn the shape and stuff carefully with wadding, making sure the wadding goes into all corners. Sew up the slit.
Shapes might be further decorated with stitches.

MAKING LINES

Rouleaux are fabric tubes which are often used in dressmaking for buttonholes and belt carriers, but they can also be used in a highly decorative way to make three-dimensional lines which when used with shapes can make pictures and patterns in high relief.

Rouleaux are made by cutting strips along the diagonal of a piece of fabric. The strip is folded lengthways and machined along the edge to make a tube and this is turned inside out. Cutting on the cross gives the tube elasticity. If the crossway strips need to be joined to make a longer tube, this can be

85 Making a rouleau.

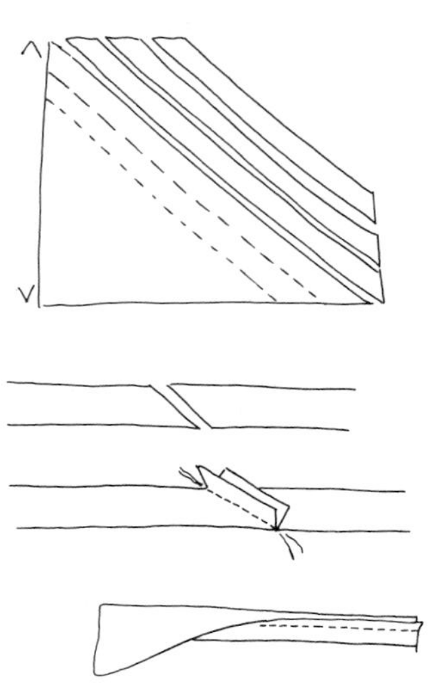

done by placing the strips at right angles to each other and machining. Rolls cannot be joined after they have been made, so work out the required length first.

Tubes can be made as thin as the process of turning inside out will allow. Quilting needles are now available which make the process much easier than the old method of using a safety pin. Firmly tie the ends of the machine thread to the eye of the quilting needle. The knot must hold, as it is very annoying if it comes undone in the middle of the process and it can be difficult to retrieve the end.

Pad the rolls with thick wool, cord, etc. Large rolls will need large bundles of wool, so to ensure that the wool does not tangle, leave both ends hanging out a little. The rolls need to be quite thick and well stuffed.

As always, it is invaluable to try out a variety of fabrics made into shapes and tubes before embarking upon a larger piece of work. See the difference between knitted and woven fabrics. Tubes can be knitted on four needles or made with french knitting or made as a strip of knitting, folded and joined. Commercial knitted fabrics can be cut into strips and will roll into tubes. Use tights, dishcloth fabrics, etc. Shiny fabrics reflect the light and transparent and translucent fabrics can be stuffed with coloured waddings and wools or with strips of metallic fabric and threads. Shoelaces, obtainable in a wide range of colours, can also be padded out and used as fabric tubes.

It is also interesting to see how the pattern on striped fabrics reacts to being made into tubes. Striped commercial fabric can be used, but it is more interesting to use fabric that is specially hand printed. Experiment by printing some fabrics along the straight grain of the fabrics, and some with the lines printed across the diagonal. Use transfer paint or crayon on synthetics or direct paint and crayons (see pages 35–8).

It is very easy to make a striped fabric by sticking lines of masking tape on plain coloured fabric and painting between the lines. When the paint is dry the tape can be removed.

As well as being used with three-dimensional fabric forms, tubes can be woven together to give an area of raised texture, or the quilting yarn used to pad out the tubes can be tightened so that the tubes gather to make ruffles. Both shapes and tubes can be ranged in lines and grids to make raised patterns and textures as well as making more representational pictures.

86 Fabric tubes made from hand printed fabric that have been gathered to create texture. (See colour plates 10 and 11.)

87 Calico Tree. Simple two-sided forms with stuffed fabric tubes.

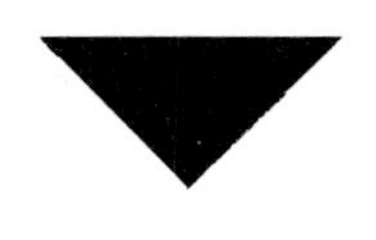

10

Making things

Quilting is functional as well as decorative. Wadded quilting produces a warm, textured fabric which is excellent for warm clothing and furnishings like bedding.

All types of quilting can be used as decoration on the various parts of a garment: cuffs, collars, hems and pockets, for example. Accessories like bags and soft jewellery can be quilted to complement an outfit.

Several points should be borne in mind when using quilting for any garment, accessory or furnishing which is to be worn or used regularly:

- All the fabrics and colourings should be washable or at least capable of being dry cleaned.
- The quilting technique employed should be functional. The stitches should be firm and well finished off and the quilting should not be so lumpy or three-dimensional that it is uncomfortable to use. Raw edges look beautiful on a wall hanging, but will not be so practical on a cushion cover.
- Any quilting should be carried out on fabric before it is finally cut out.

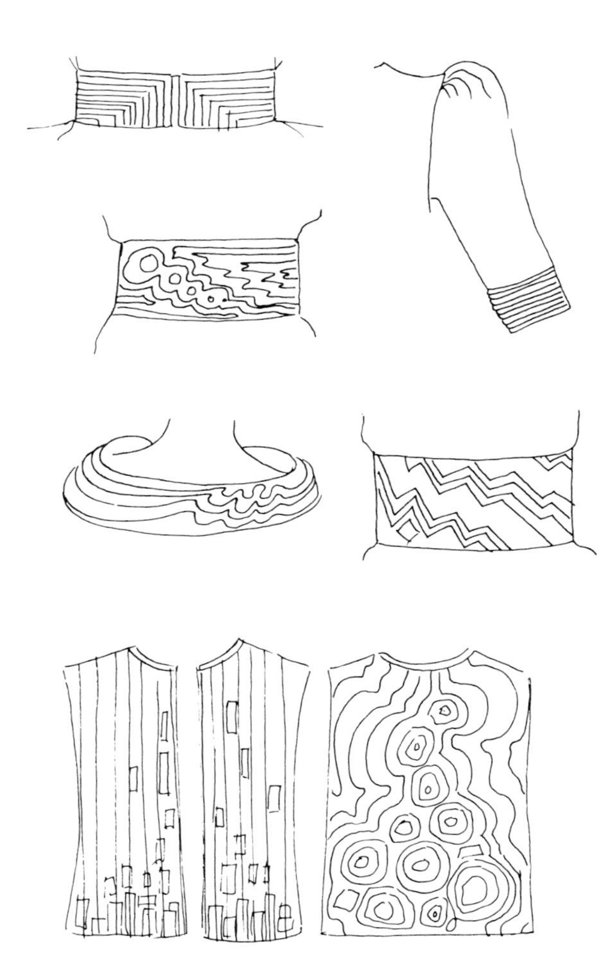

88 Items that are suitable for quilting.

CLOTHES

Choose a simple garment pattern. Before buying, make sure that the quilting design will fit onto the appropriate pattern pieces. A pattern without darts is easier to manage, unless you have enough skill to work round them.

Mark out the pattern pieces on the fabric, then

work the quilting before cutting out. This is important because the quilting might distort the fabric and pull it out of shape. When the quilting is completed, adjust the pattern pieces before cutting out.

Quilting might be added to a commercial garment to alter its appearance, with a pattern or picture on the pockets, cuffs, sleeves or body of the garment.

It is probably easiest to make a quilted pattern which can then be applied to the garment. If the actual garment itself is to be quilted, the pattern should be simple enough not to pull the garment out of shape.

FURNISHINGS

Cushion covers

Mark out the design, making sure it is on the straight grain of the fabric. Leave a good seam allowance. The zip or opening across the back of the cushion should be completed before sewing the back to the front. The cushion is then turned through the open zip. For a good finish, round the corners slightly.

Large quilts

These are easier to design and make in sections, unless you have a quilting frame. They can then be sewn up later. Leave a good seam allowance.

Join the top layer of each section by putting two pieces right side to right side and machining. Lay the quilt wrong side up on a table, and trim the wadding and backing so that each piece is just butting against the next. Lay the backing fabric over the wadding. Tack from the centre to the edges, then quilt along the seams. Trim. Turn in the edges and slipstitch.

THREE PROJECTS

Project 1: Soft containers

Quilting is excellent for small bags and purses and soft containers for gifts. Not only does the quilting look attractive, it also helps to protect what is inside.

It is important that the function of the container is carefully considered. Nothing can be more annoying than making a purse which is not quite big enough. The bags described below are all made in one piece.

1 Design the bag. Lay out on a sheet of paper the objects which the bag will contain and mark the area they cover, then make a paper bag that is the correct size by folding a sheet of paper in two and taping up the sides. Make sure everything fits. Use this as a guide.

2 Decide on the shape of the bag. Fold a sheet of paper into three to make a bag shape, deciding on the proportions of flap to sides, the width and height required, etc. Shape the base and flap roughly with a pencil. Flatten the paper out and fold in half vertically, then using your pencil mark as a guide, round off the flap and base with scissors so that the pattern is symmetrical.

89 Wadded, tied and machine quilted bag. The top layer of sticky-backed plastic traps bits of fabric and thread. The bag has a gold lining.

90 *Making a pattern for a bag.*

5 Mark out the shape of the bag and the design, but do not cut out, unless it is just to cut the fabric into a more manageable size.
6 Quilt the pattern. It is sometimes a good idea to line a quilted object so that the threads do not catch on the inside. The lining should match the quilting.
7 Sew in the zip. Cut a crossways strip of similar or contrasting fabric to go across the top edge of the purse. Machine on the right side, then turn to

92 *Machine quilted synthetic suede.*

3 Decide on the fastening. There are various possibilities: zips, buttons, press studs, velcro, etc. Decide how and when the fastening is to be added. You might prefer to leave the top open altogether. Zips should be put in before joining the sides. The bag can then be turned through the open zip.
4 The quilting design should be worked out so that it fits exactly into the area of the bag. Often, a simple quilting pattern is worked on the bag and this is then built up on the flap in a more complex form. On a bag with two sides, the front usually has more decoration than the back.

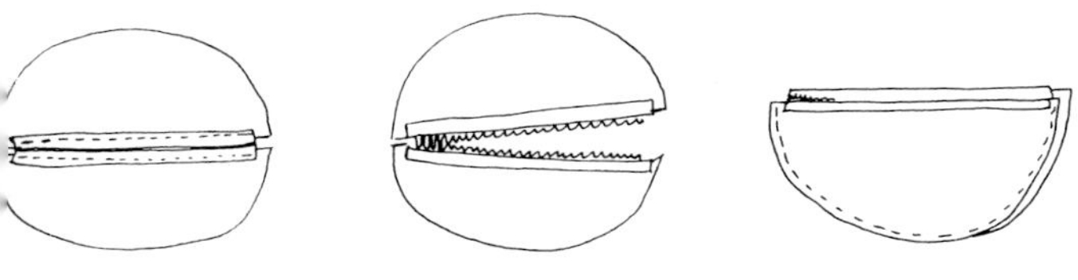

91 *Insert a zip before joining the sides of a bag or cushion.*

93 *Finishing the edges.*

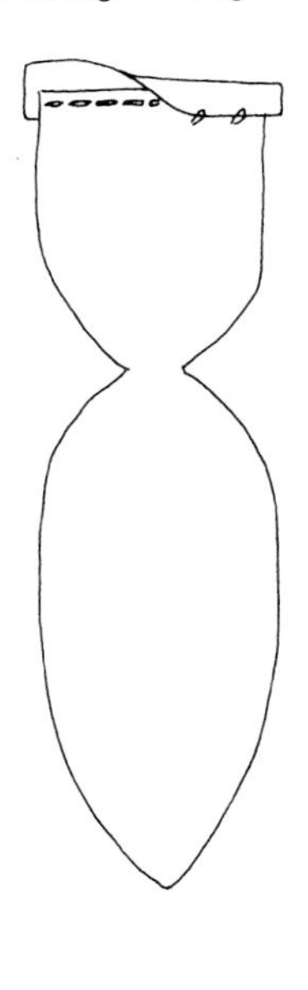

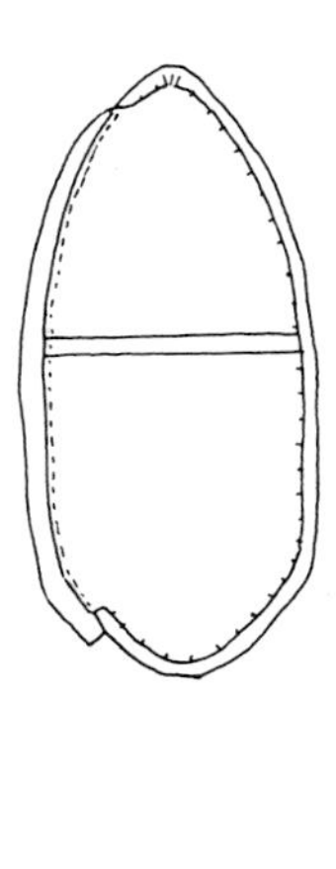

the wrong side and hem stitch. Tack in the handle, if any.
8 Cut a strip to go right round the purse, including the flap, and machine.
9 Add the fastening. This might be a toggle or bead made of the same materials, or any type of bead. Embroider a buttonhole.

Project 2: Body ornament and soft jewellery

Fabric tubes with three-dimensional fabric forms and small pieces of raised and quilted fabrics can be used together to make effective soft jewellery. Fabrics and threads are soft, pliable and colourful and can be twisted round arms, legs or neck to make decorations and jewellery which fit in with particular clothes and other accessories. Fabric is

94 Bag by Christine Cooper.

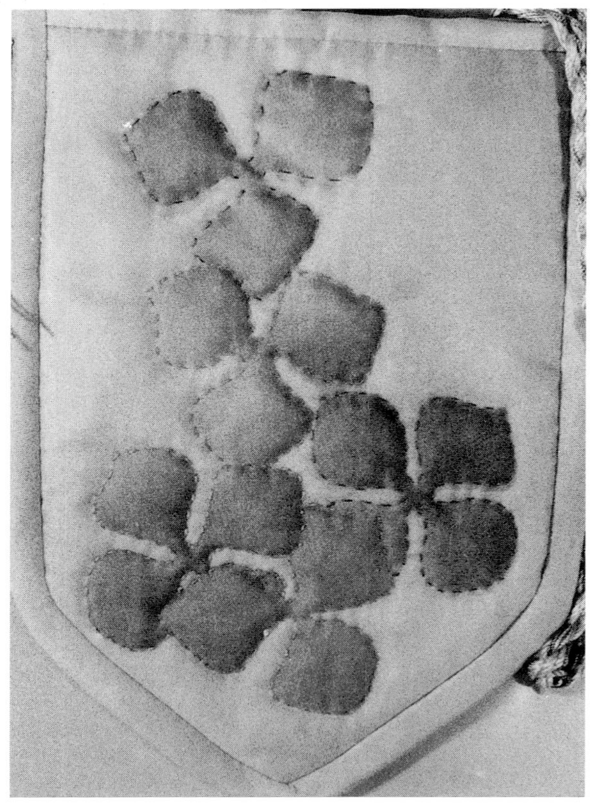

95 Bags and purses offer scope for individual design and decoration.

much cheaper than using metal so much more outrageous ornaments can be considered.

Jewellery is exotic, so choose decorative fabrics and threads which will make an impact, like silk, silk organza, gold and silver fabrics and shiny, glitzy fabric. Use gold and metallic threads, matching beads and sequins. Use plastic-coated fabrics, acetate and sticky-backed plastics with plastic tubing to go with the fabrics. Rouleaux or fabric tubes are ideal for jewellery. In general, the fabric used to make tubes should be cut on the cross.

Try out some of the following ideas:

- Make a number of tubes, which should be as thin as possible. Twist these together. Secure at each end by machining across all the tubes.
- Make a number of rouleaux and pad with wool or cord. Catch these every so often with silk threads wrapped round them all. Wrap for about 2–3 cm ($\frac{3}{4}$–$1\frac{1}{4}$ in.), perhaps in stripes, or in a contrasting thread.

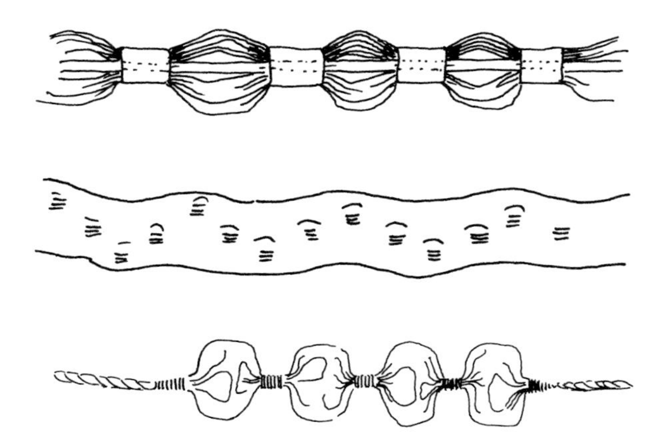

96 Designs for jewellery.

- Make a rouleau of fine fabric slightly larger than a plastic tube. Cut the plastic tube into beads. Using a cord as a central core, thread one bead inside the rouleau, then wrap the rouleau tightly with a contrasting thread and thread another plastic bead to cover it.
- Make a thick rouleau of fine, soft fabric. Every 3–4 cm ($1\frac{1}{4}$–$1\frac{1}{2}$ in.), make a line of gathering stitches round the tube. Push wadding down the tube with a knitting needle, then pull up the gathering stitches to form beads. Make sure each bead is well padded. Wrap a contrasting thread over the gathering stitches. Embroider or decorate each bead.
- Make a thick tube of a fabric like suede or shiny satin, etc. Thread a cord through and gather, so the rouleau is pushed into folds. Secure each end.

97a, b Necklace and (overleaf) earrings by Jennifer Westward. The beads are made of silk tubes which are gathered at each end and padded, then decorated with beads and sequins.

a)

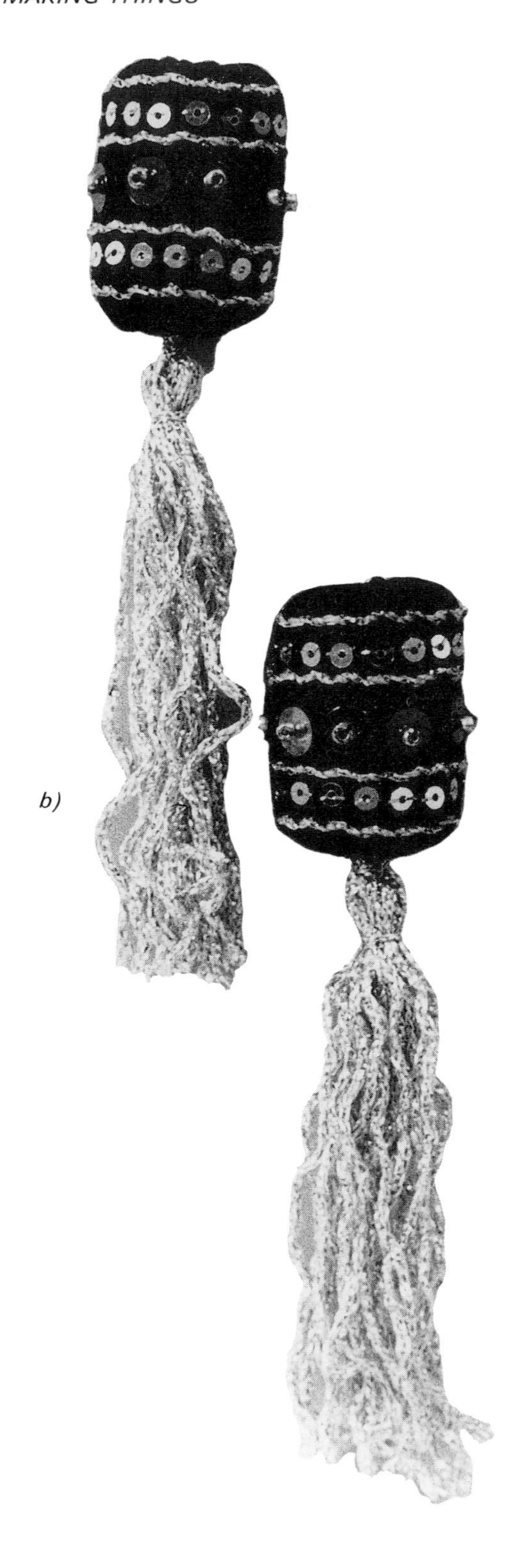
b)

- French knitting, and some shoelaces can be padded out with knitting wool.
- Wrapping. Use a core of yarns and wrap stripes of colour. Sometimes, two or three of the core threads can be brought to the surface, over the wrapping, to give a woven effect. Alternatively, use something thicker like a piece of washing line or rope. Overhand knots can be tied, or two or three wrapped threads can be caught together every so often.

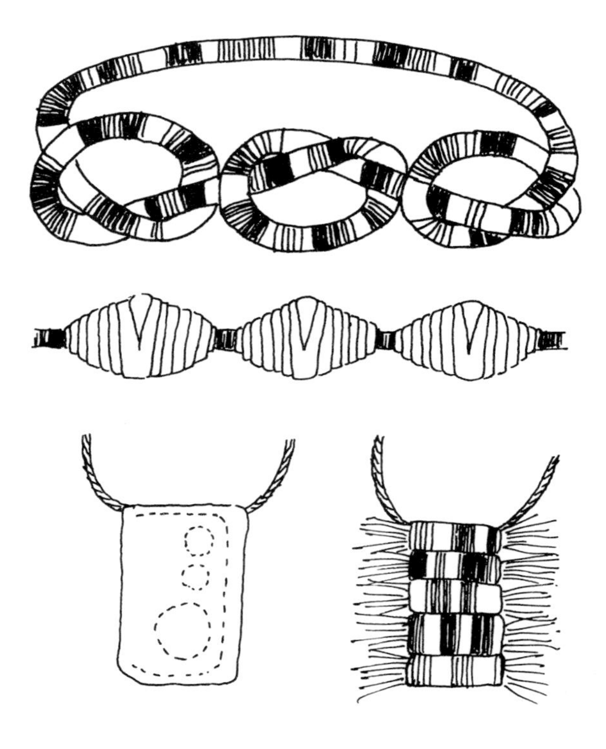

98 Beads and forms for jewellery can be made in a variety of ways.

- Soft beads. These can be made with a small length of fabric tube about 4 cm ($1\frac{1}{2}$ in.) long. Turn in and gather the ends, stuff and embroider.
- Make beads by winding a long triangle or strip of felt round a plastic drinking straw. Spread glue along the length of the felt, wind evenly and leave to dry. These beads can be decorated with woven bars by wrapping thread round the bead and weaving on the wrapping thread. Thread on cord or hang on an earring.

99 Earrings by Geraldine Prince.

- Make three-dimensional quilted forms (see pages 58–61) which can be hung about the neck on a cord or on an earring. These can be made in materials like plastic, suede or plasticized fabric as well as silk and satin and calico. Simple quilted forms based on triangles, squares and rectangles or flower and leaf shapes are very attractive.

Finishings and fastenings

These are very important and have to be considered at the same time as the design of the jewellery. Fasteners for metal jewellery are available at craft shops, or a hook and eye can be made from wire and covered with yarn. These can be attached to the length of decoration as the end is finished off.

Machine across the ends of any fabric tubes to hold in position and prevent fraying. Sew the fastening to the machine stitches and cover the gap with wrapped yarn or a collar of fabric.

Some decorations look better when simply tied with a cord, or fastened with a loop and fabric bead.

To make a twisted cord The finished cord is about a third of the length of the yarns used. Use smooth yarns like silk and metallic machine embroidery yarns, tapestry wools, stranded cottons, etc. Rug wool or double knitting wool can be used for really thick cords.

1 Measure the yarn. You will need several lengths, about three times as long as the finished cord.

2 Double the yarns, holding the looped end with a nail or a drawing pin. Tie a knot near the end and, using a pencil or knitting needle, twist the yarn until it is tight and starts to twist over itself.

3 Double the yarn back over itself smoothly, and tie the ends together (this is important, as otherwise the cord will spring apart). One end of the cord has a knot and the other can be used as a loop. The knot can be decorated to make a tassel, then used as a fastening.

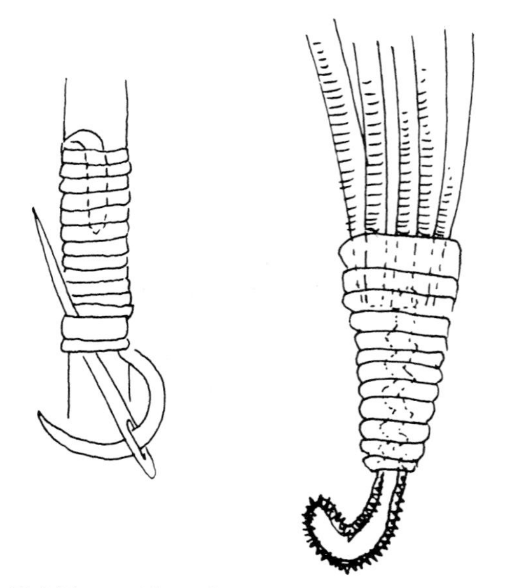

100 Finishing and fastening techniques.

101 Dolls around the world.
(a) Egyptian paddle-shaped doll, about 2000 BC. Clay pellets for hair.
(b) Harlequin. Jointed cardboard doll.
(c) Japanese traditional dolls (modern).
(d) Russian dolls.
(e) Carved gourds from Peru.

Project 3: Figures and dolls

From the earliest times people have been making figures and dolls from materials like wood, leather and fabrics, not only to comfort children but also to use as mascots and in magic and religious ceremonies. Traces of these figures can still be seen preserved in museums.

Modern people are no less superstitious and even today mascots have a very strong appeal – witness the mascots and dolls which dangle in the windows of cars and the dolls which are taken to all kinds of competition between rival teams.

The particular figures described here are based on the doll patterns which are sold with the back and the front already printed on fabric, ready to be cut out and sewn. They are also influenced by the simple primitive shapes of dolls and mascots from all over the world. There is much scope for individual research, ideas and design in a project like this. The success of the method lies in using a simple overall shape and filling in details either with paint or surface embroidery. A basic triangle or rectangle with rounded corners, or an oval, can all be used to enclose a more complicated figure. The figure should be easy to turn inside out and to pad. The figure described in this project stands about 20 cm (8 in.) high, but figures can be any size. It is as well to remember that very small figures are much more difficult to manage.

Begin by designing a figure on paper. It is easier to achieve a symmetrical figure by drawing on a folded paper, drawing just half the shape to the fold. Then cut out.

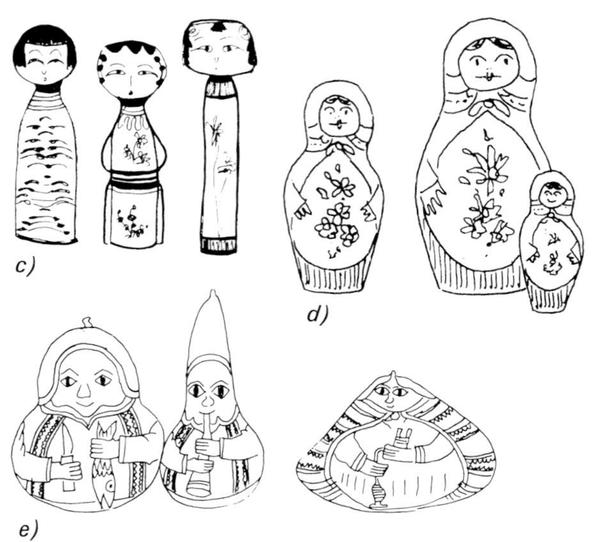

102 Hand painted, machine embroidered dolls on sailcloth.

Draw round the paper shape twice on a piece of closely woven fabric such as cotton, poplin or calico, leaving at least 4 cm ($1\frac{1}{2}$ in.) between the figures and from the edge, for turnings. *Do not cut out at this stage.*

The details of the figure can then be planned on paper. Start with a face and perhaps the position of the hands, if any, and the areas of colour and pattern which will indicate the clothes. Transfer these to the fabric and paint or pattern with colour, with the sewing machine, or by hand.

It might be that a more complicated body profile can be drawn within the simple outside shape; the space between can then be painted in a dark colour so that it will recede into the background and the eye will be caught by the more intricate shape.

Not only standing figures, but figures in action, animals, birds and fish, trees and buildings can be made in this way. This type of figure avoids the complication of trying to design shapings and gussets which are not always successful. By using a simple shape and depending on colour and decoration for impact, the end product is much more likely to be effective.

When the figures are decorated, they can be cut out, leaving a seam allowance of at least 1.5–2 cm ($\frac{1}{2}$–$\frac{3}{4}$ in.). Place right sides together and machine, leaving a gap for the wadding. Cut curves as described above and trim corners. Turn.

Pack the figure with wadding, stuffing or kapok, making sure the stuffing is packed in tight in all the corners – use the knob end of a knitting needle. Figures always look much better if they are well stuffed.

The shapes can be decorated with hair, accessories and so on, but because these figures depend on a simple primitive shape for their beauty, do not be tempted to spoil this with too much extra embellishment after the main figure is finished. Rather, try to incorporate all the patterning within the main shape.

All manner of pictures and patterns in three dimensions and high relief can be constructed by putting together simply made forms and fabric tube lines.

103 The basic shape of a doll. (See colour plate 13.)

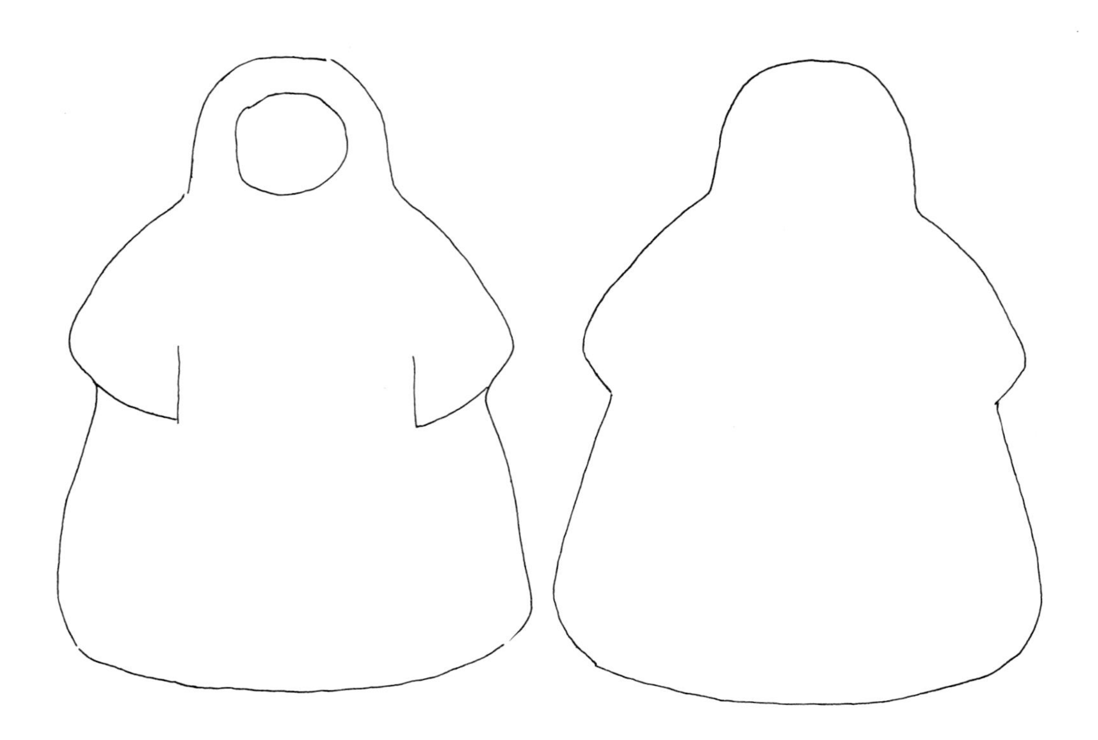

104 *Dolls from Peru. These dolls are made from textiles found in graves which had been looted for their pottery. 'The materials, almost certainly pre-Columbian (AD1000-1500) are left over from looting, and are more saleable as dolls than as fragments of textiles. The dolls are therefore fairly recent – probably originally made from twigs bound with thread (both arms and legs), and straw and twigs for the body. Patterned material is often used for the face and head.'* (Handout from Global Village Crafts Ltd)

105 *A group can be made in a similar way to those shown in Figure 104 with a felt roll, the top folded over for the head and tied, and the face covered with knitted fabric. The clothes are made from samples of pulled thread embroidery which were done initially as experiments.*

Part Two

USING OTHER MATERIALS TO RAISE A SURFACE

11

Stiffening fabrics

Wadding and padding are only two of the materials which can be used to create a raised surface. Materials like card give a much harder, more angular surface and there are many more materials which give a variety of different finishes.

Many of the materials like wire, wood, paper and glue, are traditional. Materials like plastic are new. It is a good idea to explore each in turn to see what can be achieved.

Fabrics used for tailoring, like canvas and tarlatan, are stiffened to give shape to collars and facings, and stiffened shapes are used as a basis for the construction of some hats, but this technique can be used in a much more creative way to raise a surface and make an interesting and exciting texture or three-dimensional form. This surface can then be embroidered, or incorporated into a piece of embroidery as a raised shape. Completely three-dimensional forms can also be constructed and decorated with colour, fabric and embroidery.

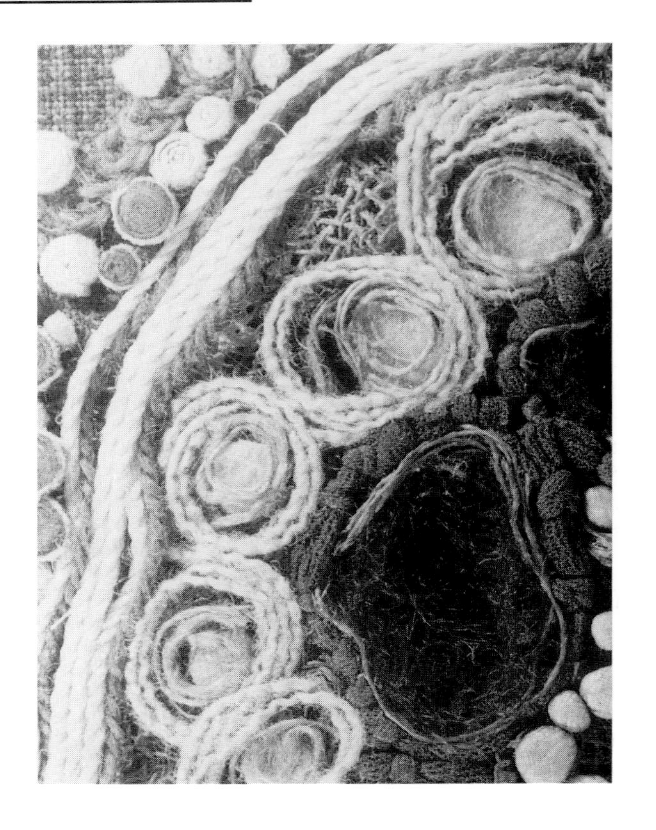

106 Glue-stiffened fabrics and threads.

STIFFENING AGENTS

PVA glue and wallpaper paste are recommended to begin with, as they are easy and safe to use, but for anyone who is particularly interested in pursuing the technique in more detail, it is worth trying out more unusual agents like glue size, varnishes of various types, spray starches, polishes like furniture polish and waxes like beeswax. All of these will stiffen fabrics to a greater or lesser degree and all give a look that is unique to the agent used.

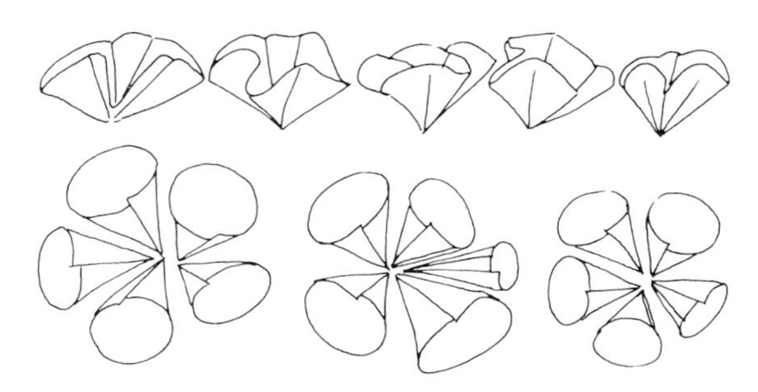

107 Stiffened fabric can be shaped and folded.

PVA glue

Sold as an all-purpose, water-based glue under various trade names, this is especially useful as it can be used either neat, to hold thick fabrics in position, or diluted with water, when it can be used just to stiffen a fabric, rather than to harden it. The glue sold for stiffening fabric blinds is based on PVA.

Before planning a complicated project, experiment to see how different materials react to different treatments. Suitable fabrics are natural fabrics which crease easily like tarlatan, cottons, sailcloth, muslins, calico, hessian, etc. which are very easy to use, and there are many natural and synthetic mixes which can also be tried out. Only a few synthetics, like nylon net for example, are particularly difficult. It is a good idea to try out small samples of a wide range of fabrics, made from both synthetic and natural fibres. Keep experiments for reference.

Begin by dipping some of the sample fabrics into 100% PVA glue, allow to dry, then iron. Go on to try other proportions of water and glue, for example two parts water to one part glue, one part glue to one part water, etc. Peg the wet sample fabrics on a line to drip dry and turn every few minutes so that the glue has a chance to run through all the fibres. Iron when dry. The fabric will be stiff, depending on the proportions of glue used. The glue prevents the fabric from fraying, and fabric can be folded and will hold its shape. Cut shapes like circles and squares, then fold and cut to make texture.

108 Glue-stiffened fabrics can be manipulated in a variety of ways and hold their shape.

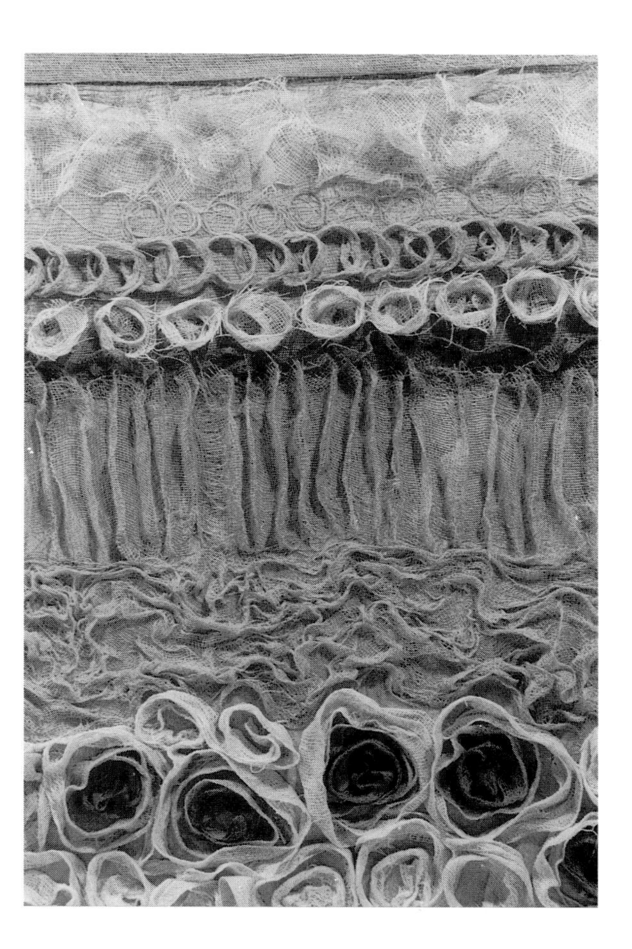

Wallpaper paste

Both starch and cellulose pastes are suitable, and should be mixed following the instructions on the packet. To mix a smaller amount, use fractions of the quantities recommended, but be as accurate as possible, as too much powder will give a very thick paste which is inclined to go lumpy. Lightweight and heavy fabrics can be compared with similar weight wallpapers.

DIPPING

Fabrics can be completely dipped in wallpaper paste or 100% PVA. Squeeze out the excess paste, although the fabric should still be wet. Yarns can also be used. Spread the fabrics and threads on a plastic work surface and push into pleats, swirls gathers and textures, using a large needle or tweezers. Any extra colour could be added at this stage using water-based fabric paints.

Fabrics can also be looped to make arches; strips of fabric can be pleated together or several layers of fabric stood on edge, and so on. Keep a bowl of water nearby to rinse the hands. Allow the manipulated fabrics to dry completely on the work surface. They will not stick to plastic and when dry can be peeled off and applied to another surface. It is easy to sew through the stiffened fabric.

If the textures are to be constructed directly onto a permanent background, this must be prepared first. Soak the background fabric in the paste and smooth onto a rigid base, like cardboard or polystyrene, tucking the edges underneath. Leave this to dry. The glue is likely to pull the background and distort it slightly. This can be rectified in most cases by glueing a piece of similar fabric to the back of the card or polystyrene base.

109 Stiffened fabric layers (a) stood on edge, and (b) folded, by Sheila Leech.

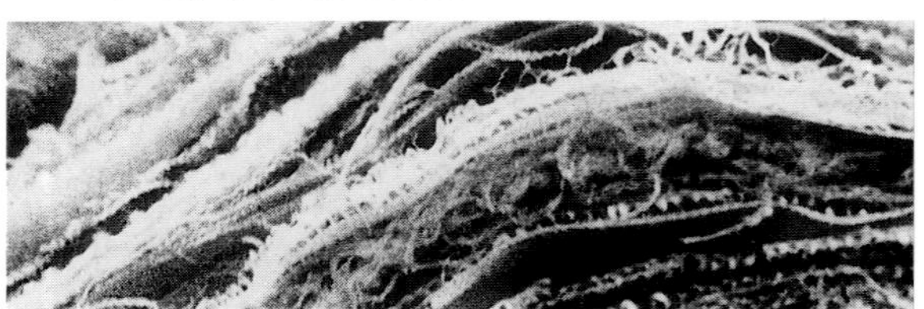

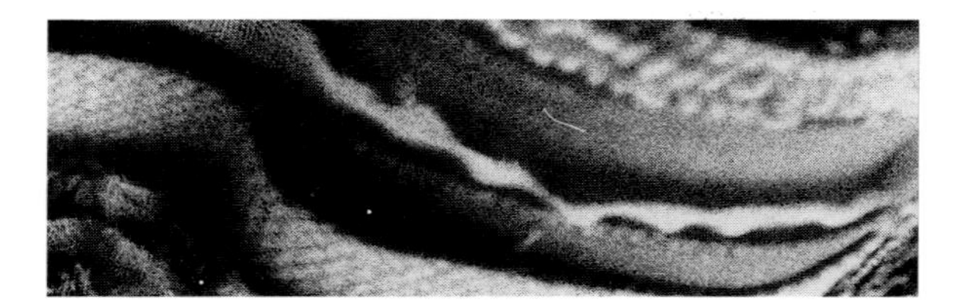

ROLLING AND FOLDING

Because fabric is a flexible medium, it can be rolled and folded into shapes and forms straight onto a prepared background, or manipulated and then applied to another piece of work. Experiment by cutting strips of fabric on the straight grain of the fabric or on the cross and rolling into tubes. Go on to rolling several different colours or different widths of fabric together, or use frayed or torn fabrics, and roll these. If the fabrics are rolled round a knitting needle, the resulting forms can be used like beads. The dried shapes can be slashed with a craft knife to reveal the colour of fabrics underneath. Heavy fabrics like hessian can be dipped in paste and moulded into figure shapes and squares of fabric can be folded into cones which might then be used as a basis for further decoration.

110 Rolled and folded fabric shapes.

MOULDING

Fabric can be used to mould a form in the same way as paper is used in papier-mâché. Curved or rounded shapes can be made by using the side of a bucket or the bottom of a shallow bowl as a mould. Foil can be shaped into a mould, or kitchen foil containers can be used. *Protect the mould with plastic film.*

Simple three-dimensional objects of all kinds can be moulded by covering smooth objects like pebbles, eggs, a shallow bowl or a fruit with glue-soaked fabrics, then removing when dry.

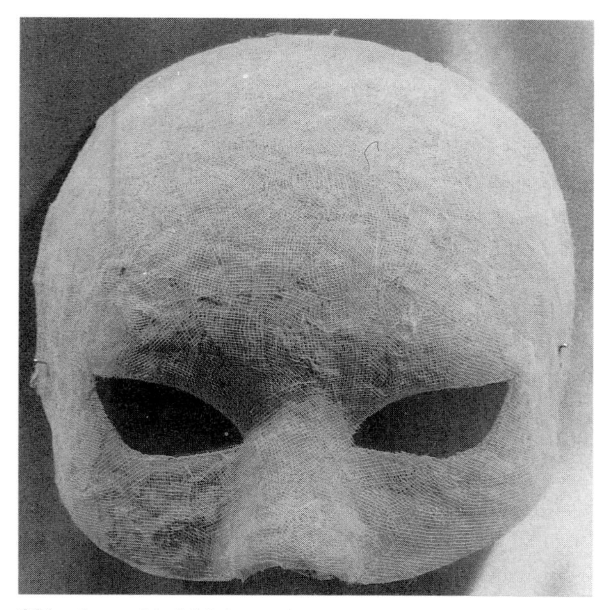

111 A moulded fabric mask.

112 Form moulded on a cardboard Easter egg using tarlatan. Decorated with stitches, beads, braids and lined with silk.

PROJECT: STONES AND PEBBLES

Many people find the beautiful pebbles on the beach fascinating and there must be many gardens which have a collection of sea-worn pebbles brought home from a seaside holiday. These are easy to mould because they have such simples shapes.

1 Choose a reasonably large, smooth pebble.

2 Protect the stone with a layer of plastic film (normally used in the kitchen).

3 Decide now how you eventually intend to remove the stiffened form. This can be done either by covering the stone in two halves, so that a split is left round the middle of the mould, or by cutting through the fabric when it has dried, with a sharp craft knife.

4 Tear or cut strips of fine fabric like tarlatan or muslin, dip in the paste and wrap, or bandage the stone, building up at least five layers of fabric. The strips can be bandaged in different directions to give the form extra strength. The last layer might be a patchwork of coloured fabrics, or the shape might be coloured with fabric paint while it is still wet.

5 Leave to dry thoroughly. If the fabric is removed while it is still damp, it will collapse.

6 Remove the moulded fabric. If it is made in two halves, mark exactly where they are to join. If you use a craft knife, it should be sharp.

7 The two sides can then be joined up. This needs to be done carefully, and bit by bit, pasting wet patches of fabric across the join. Let each section dry before going on to the next, or the whole thing may collapse.

The shape can be filled with sawdust or sand to give weight, or just left as a shell. If the shape is to be filled, join the edges almost all the way round, leaving a small opening. Cut a star from the opening, to hold a funnel, and pour in sawdust.

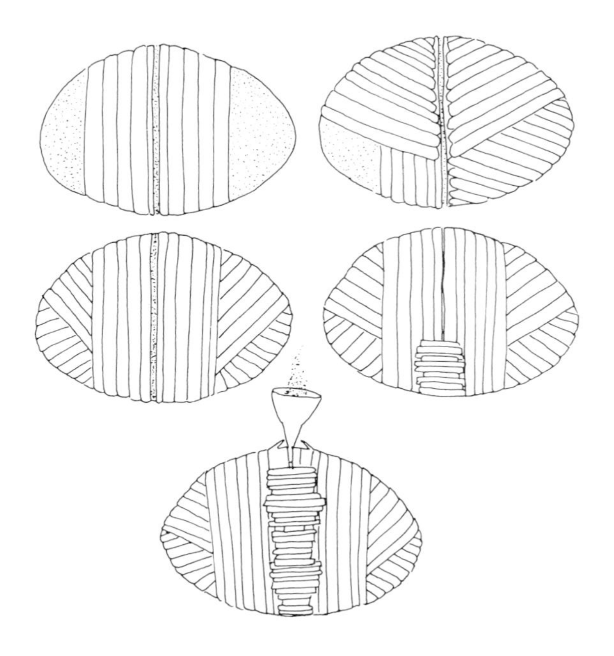

These fabric moulds look beautiful in themselves, but there are various ways of adding further decoration, if necessary. *Remember*, though, that the shapes will collapse if they are wetted, so any glue used from now on must be either spirit- or latex-based.

- A pattern of fabric shapes or yarns might be stuck on to create a surface pattern.
- Small crocheted or raised embroidery shapes might be used.
- The shape can be covered with fabric, then embroidered. It is easier to cover a rounded shape by bandaging it with fine fabric cut on the cross or with fine stretch fabric. Catch the fabric down as you go along, cutting off any excess material. The fabric can then be used as a base for applying pieces of hand embroidery, machine embroidery, knitting and crochet, or for attaching surface weaving or raised stitches.
- Spray with car paint in a well-ventilated room.

113 Steps in moulding a stone or pebble.

114 Pebble moulding. Note the plastic film covering the stone. The small crocheted shapes will be used to decorate the finished stone.

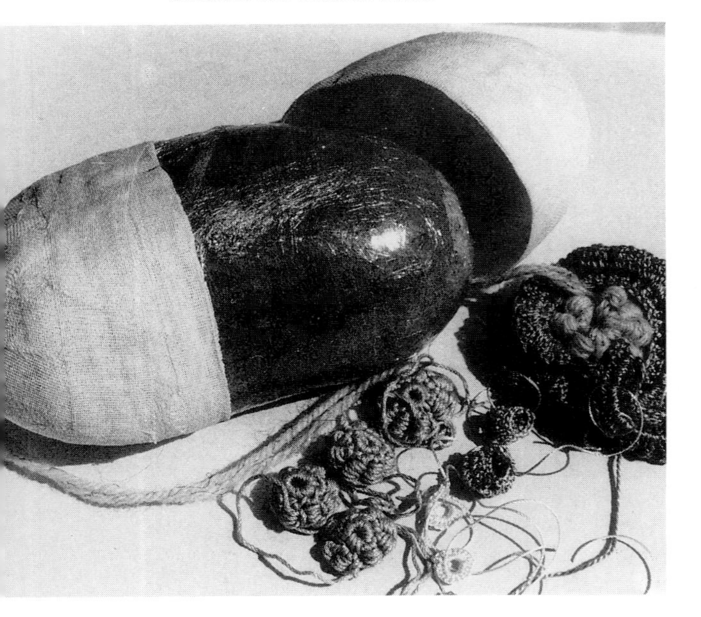

115 Three forms decorated with a collage of coton perlé and soft cotton yarns stuck on with latex-based glue.

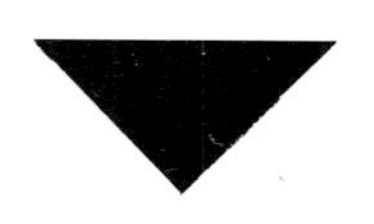

12

Stiffening with card

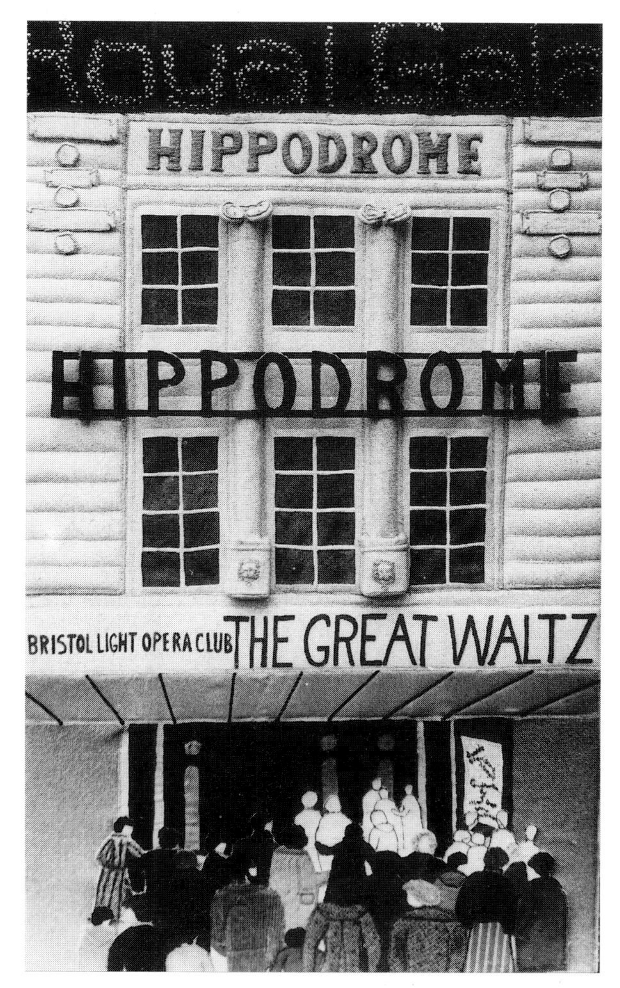

116 Bristol Hippodrome by Alison Sutton. Card is particularly successful as a 'raising agent' when depicting buildings.

Card used instead of wadding to raise a textile surface gives a pleasing hard finish with a crisp line. Card, paper hardboard, and pelmet vilene can also be successfully used as a light, rigid base on which to build layers of wadding and can be used to support fabric shapes which are built up to make rigid three-dimensional forms. Card shapes covered with fabric are easy to sew together.

It is always a good idea to use fairly simple shapes, which are much easier to cover successfully. A more complicated shape can almost always be broken down into a group of simple, more manageable shapes. The weight of the card should be chosen to fit in with what is being made.

METHODS OF WORKING WITH CARD

Lacing is used where glue might spoil the look and finish of an object. It is much easier to glue round an uneven, curved edge and wrapping is much more successful on a shape with parallel sides. It is sometimes necessary to use more than one method on a complicated piece of work.

You sometimes need to bend a piece of card, for example when making the side of a round box. Card and thick paper bend much more easily in one direction than in the other. Try bending the card in both directions before deciding how to cut it. It can be bent more easily round a tin or a rounded surface. Some cards are much easier to bend than others. It sometimes helps to dampen the card very slightly. Butt the two ends together onto masking tape. Cover the card with fabric.

Lacing a rectangle

1 Cut the card shape with a sharp craft knife. Edges need to be completely smooth so that no uneven nibs show through fine fabrics.
2 Iron the fabric and cut so that the straight grain of the fabric is parallel with the edge of the card. The fabric should be about 10 mm ($\frac{3}{8}$ in.) wider than the card all round.
3 To prevent fraying and pulling, either sew zigzag stitches along the edges of the fabric with a sewing machine, or make a single turning.
4 Lay the card on the fabric and, working from the middle, pull the edges over the card by taking alternate stitches from opposite sides. Work loosely from the centre to the edges, tying on further sewing threads rather than finishing off each one and starting again. Pull into shape by tightening the stitches. Tuck in the corners and stitch across. The effect should be smooth like a drum, but not tight enough to pull the card.
5 If the rectangle has been bent into a circle, make sure the covering is taut by measuring carefully, then join the fabric with machine stitching before lacing as above.

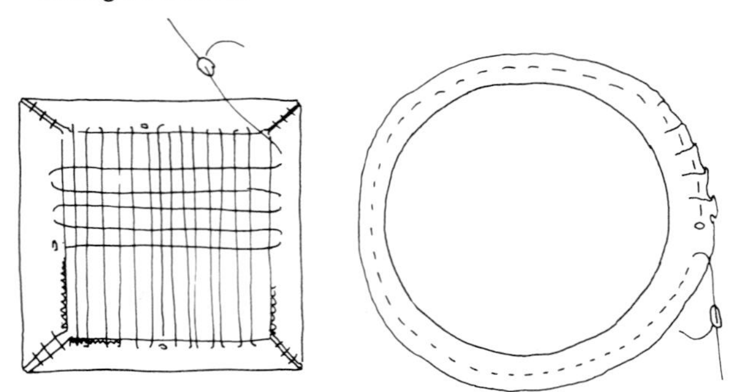

117 Methods of covering card.

Lacing a circle

Cut the card circle, and the fabric slightly larger, as above. Starting with a knot, make a line of running stitches parallel to the edge of the card and about 5 mm ($\frac{1}{4}$ in.) away. Pull up these stiches to enclose the card shape. Finish off securely.

Covering both sides of a shape

Sometimes you need to cover a shape, e.g. a rectangle of card, on both sides, perhaps with a different fabric on each side. This is easy to do by making a pocket of cloth, inserting the card, and turning in and sewing up the end.

118 Card and paper shapes enclosed in fabric and assembled as a flowerhead.

1 Cut out the back and front with the warp and weft of the fabric cut on the straight.
2 Sew round three sides with right sides facing. Turn.
3 Put in the card, which should fit as snugly as possible without bending. Turn in the end and stitch across.
4 Several rectangles of the same width can be similarly enclosed in a long pocket of fabric, and separated by a line of machine stitches worked as near as possible to the card (use the zipper foot). Each line of stitches makes a hinge. This method can be used to make simple rectangular box shapes.
5 It is possible to go on to use several strips of card, contained within a pocket of fabric in the same way, to make a flexible shape, which might be used for a gusset to join two other shapes. Make sure the strips of card and the fabric are cut and sewn accurately, to give a good fit.

Glueing

Use a glue which is compatible with card and fabric and read the instructions before proceeding as some glued surfaces need to be left for a few minutes before being pressed together, while others stick immediately.

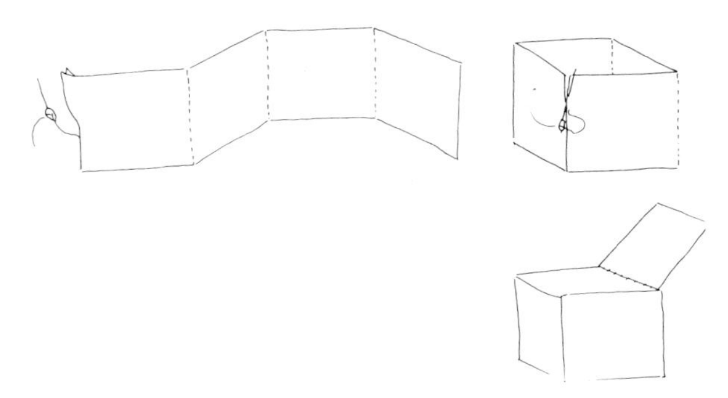

119 Construction of a simple square or rectangular box.

1 Iron the fabric. Notice which way the warp and weft of the fabric run and how this might affect the look of the finished work. A piece of work made up of several covered shapes might be spoiled if the straight grain of one is either out of true or goes in the opposite direction to the others.
2 Lay the card shape on the wrong side of the fabric. To prevent possible fraying and for added strength, draw round the card on the fabric with a dissolvable fabric marker, and machine stitch along the line. Cut notches on any concave edges, and slits into a convex edge up to the stitches, but be careful not to cut them.
3 Apply glue sparingly as directed. Press the fabric over the card. Occasionally the pull of fabric on only one side of a large card shape distorts it. If this happens and if it is important to keep the card flat, glue a similar but slightly smaller shape to the wrong side.
4 Card can also be covered with fabric which has been soaked in PVA or wallpaper paste, and a pattern of cut card shapes might first be glued to the card to create a raised pattern on the surface.

120 Use a fabric 'pocket' to construct a flexible shape.

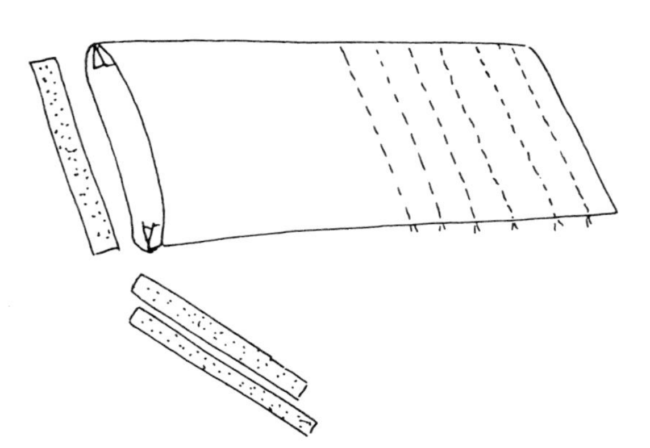

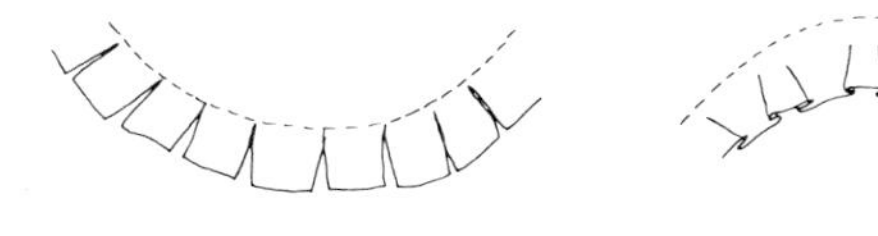

121 Cut slits (convex edge) and notches (concave edges) on curved edges to fit snugly.

Padding a card surface

Sometimes the surface of the card needs to be padded with wadding, felt or foam to give a softer, more domed effect.

Cut the wadding slightly smaller than the card and tease out the edges. Two or three layers of wadding should be cut so that each piece is slightly smaller than the one underneath.

Spread a very thin layer of glue on the card, and press on the first layer of wadding. The wadding itself will hold any subsequent pieces. Allow glue to dry thoroughly before proceeding.

Knitted fabrics can be used, particularly over wadding and card, as they are very flexible.

The methods described here, or a combination of methods, can be used to cover almost any card shape with fabric. It is possible to build up large three-dimensional and rigid objects by combining various shapes and by sewing the edges together with ladder stitch.

When making a construction, it is essential to plan carefully, and to experiment on a small scale. Make a paper and sticky-tape model, if necessary, and write down each problem as it arises and work out

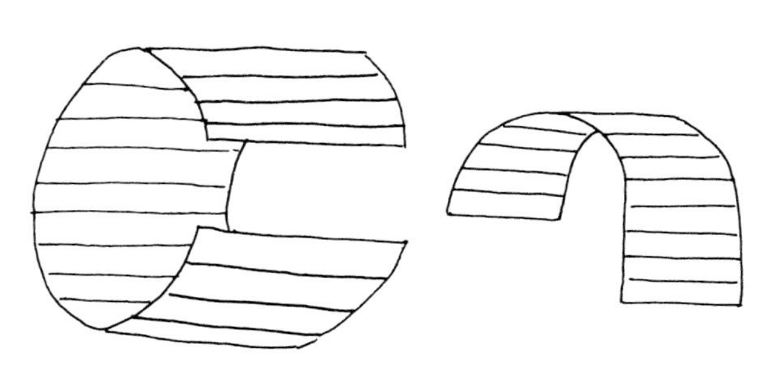

122 Original sketch of Totterdown, Bristol, which was the inspiration for a card and fabric quilted panel. (See colour plate 16.)

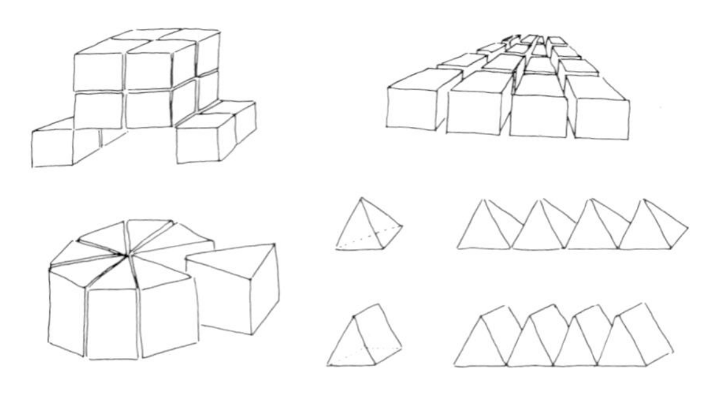

123 Small shapes can be built up into larger constructions.

how it is to be solved before proceeding. It is very depressing to make something and find at the last minute that something has been forgotten which should have been added at an earlier stage.

Wrapping card

This is an interesting technique, using shapes with parallel sides, like strips, rectangles, etc. A simple rectangle can be wrapped, making a decorative surface in itself, but a more complicated surface can be made by wrapping strips individually, then assembling them in a block.

It is possible to hide the ends of the strips behind a mount, but they might also be attached to the front of a mount, sometimes to greater effect. Colour

124 Little Red Car. Sides and base are of covered card. Fabric strip gusset from back to front bumper. Card wheels, padded and covered with painted, machine embroidered wheel pattern. The wheels are attached with Velcro spots.

the protruding ends of the strips with paint or crayons to match the wrapping threads.

Wrapping a strip of card with yarn is easier to do if a strip of double-sided sticky tape is placed down the back of the card to hold the threads in position.

There are many ways of using this simple technique, which can be stunningly effective.

- The yarns used can be smooth or textured, but as each gives quite a different effect, try them out beforehand.
- Card strips can be cut all the same width or in different widths, all the same length or different lengths. The strips can be arranged in parallel lines, at angles to each other, arranged in blocks, or woven together They can be arranged at angles, to give a raised surface.
- Blocks can be of contrasting or analogous colours in an abstract pattern, or in colours ranging from light to dark, through the tones of one colour. A wrapping of a representational painting or photograph is interesting to do and gives an attractive impressionistic picture.

PROJECT: A WRAPPED LANDSCAPE

To begin, choose a picture, a photograph or a painting which is composed of fairly simple shapes.

1 Choose the yarns, which should match as nearly as possible the colours in the picture.

2 Trace the picture, marking areas of colour and texture.

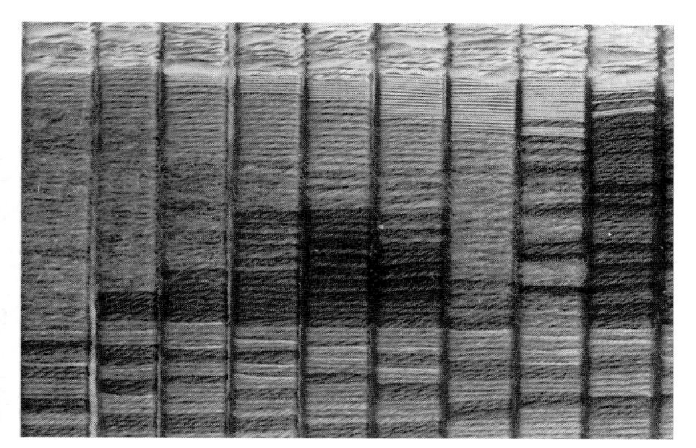

125 Detail of wrapped landscape pictures. (See colour plate 18.)

3 Have the tracing enlarged to the required size.
4 Select a piece of mounting card the same size as the photocopy.
5 Turn over the photocopy and go over the lines with a soft pencil. Place the photocopy right side up on the card, and go over the lines with a hard pencil to transfer the lines to the card.
6 Colour in the areas of colour.
7 Cut the card into equal strips with a steel ruler and a craft knife.
8 Number the pieces so that they can be reassembled in the right order.
9 Stick a strip of double-sided sticky tape down the back of each piece.
10 Wrap each piece according to the colour on the card, gradually peeling off the top layer of tape as you proceed. If there is an equal amount of two colours at any time, alternate the same two colours of yarn, and so on.
11 When all the pieces are wrapped, arrange them on another background card and stick the pieces down using double-sided sticky tape.

Variations

Use other materials for wrapping instead of card: rope or cord, plastic-coated washing line, plastic rods and tubing, dowelling, etc.

126 Method of making a wrapped picture.

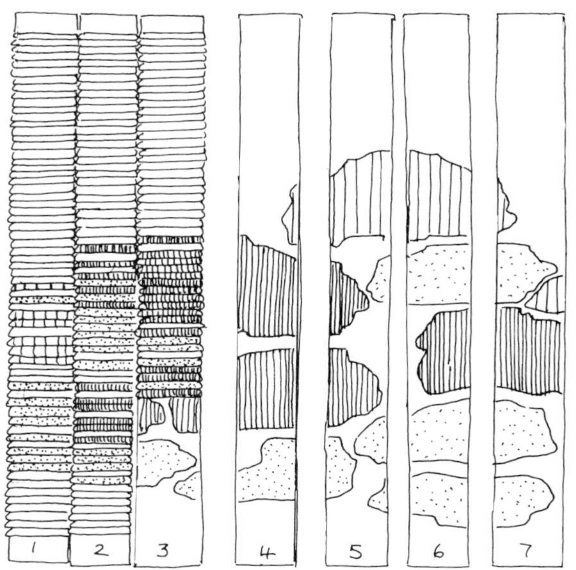

13

Stiffening with wire

127 Headdress for Notting Hill Carnival.

128 Little Plant. Jewellery wire is zigzag stitched onto fabric which is then cut into leaf shapes. The leaves are stuck into modelling clay.

Wire was commonly used to stiffen clothing until only a few years ago when garment shapes became much more simple. Wiring is still used in the theatre and for fantastic carnival costumes and is also used for supporting fabric forms like lampshades and in upholstery.

One of the unique properties of wired fabrics is the fact that the fabric can be bent into various shapes, and will hold in that position. Not only can a fabric be stiffened with wire, but wires can be covered with threads. Wire bases or armatures can be created making a strong, lightweight form which can then be padded and covered with fabric.

WIRE TO USE WITH FABRICS AND THREADS

Wire is manufactured in a great variety of weights ranging from fine silver jeweller's wire and fuse wire to cable used in the building industry. For textiles it is best to use the finest wire possible to support the fabric.

Wire is surprisingly strong, particularly if several parallel rows of wire are used. Experiment with wire which is available around the house at first, to explore the possibilities, then go on from there. Plastic-covered wire used to tie plants in the garden is easy to cover or sew onto fabric but obviously very fine wire would be more suitable for a fragile silk muslin and a thicker wire for a larger-scale sculpture.

Fuse wire, garden wire, etc. are available at ironmongers' and DIY shops, and silver wire can be bought from specialist craft suppliers. There are specialist wire suppliers who advertise in the Yellow Pages and who keep a wide range of wire of all kinds. Even pipe cleaners and wire tags for plastic bags are useful for small effects. Chicken wire can be used to make more rounded shapes and plastic-covered wire mesh makes an interesting grid which can be used as a basis for fabric and stitches. Wire lampshade rings will support weaving and detached embroidery stitches.

WORKING WITH WIRE

Although some wire is easy to bend by hand, more accurate shapes can be achieved by using two pairs of pliers: one to hold the wire, the other to bend it into position. The pliers should be a suitable size for the gauge of wire you are working with, and jewellery pliers are very good for working with fine and medium gauge wire, or use two small pairs of domestic pliers.

It is sometimes easier to use two pieces of wire twisted together rather than a thicker wire. Try not to bend wire too many times in the same place, or it will be weakened. Use wire cutters for cutting ends, not scissors.

SOME METHODS FOR COVERING WIRE

Using a sewing machine

1 This is very easy to do on a swing needle sewing machine. Use a zigzag stitch and loosen the top tension slightly as for buttonholing. The width of the stitch is determined by the thickness of the wire and the stitch length should be a close zigzag rather than a satin stitch. It is better to go over the wire twice.

2 Start working about halfway along the wire, stitch to one end then down the whole length of the wire, turn and stitch back to where you started. These covered wires can be made into simple forms by twisting them together.

3 Fabrics can be attached to the wire with satin stitch. These can then be cut, torn or frayed out to make feather and leaf shapes. Look at leaves and feathers to see how they are constructed with a central support which holds them in position.

129 Fabric feathers.

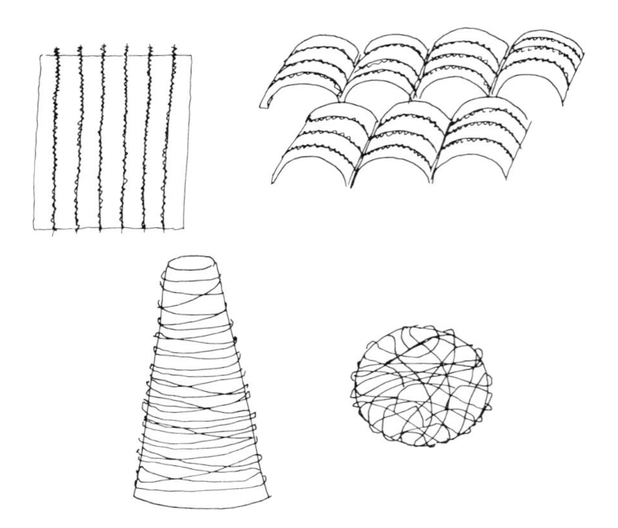

130 Wire provides the means to experiment with shaped fabric.

4 A whole area of fabric can be wired, then bent into a shape. Sew the wire with a close zigzag stitch. Experiment by sewing parallel pieces of wire across a fabric, then see the effect of bending the shape in different directions.

It is easy to see the possibilities of varying the patterns of the lines of wire and also of sewing wires through several layers of fabrics, cutting some away to reveal those underneath, or leaving pieces to hang off (see Chapter 8).

For a crisper finish, lightly stiffen the fabrics by dipping in PVA glue, and press. Sets of the same shape (squares, rectangles, triangles, etc.) might be wired in the same pattern, then arranged together to make an area of repeated pattern.

5 Padded shapes can be attached by leaving the ends of the threads used to make the shape. These can then be caught in the machine stitching.

6 Wire can also be incorporated into a rouleau. Wrap the wire firmly in strips of muslin, wrapped round wadding if necessary, so that the wire shape is just a little smaller than the diameter of the rouleau, but can be pushed through without unravelling.

Experiment with a variety of different fabrics and materials.

By hand

Wire can simply be covered by wrapping a yarn tightly round it either in one colour or in stripes. Bend the end of the wire over so that the thread does not fall off the end. Blanket stitch, or the half hitch which is used in macramé, can be used to make a decorative surface. Any stitch which is worked over a core can be used for covering wire.

Any hand or machine embroidery to be incorporated should all be done before the wire is sewn on. Plan where decoration, fabrics and wires are to go before beginning, so that all the stages can be carried out in the right order. Always try to work with simple shapes, building these together to make a final form rather than trying to make something so complicated that it cannot work.

MAKING THREE-DIMENSIONAL FORMS WITH WIRE

Larger and more complicated forms or a complete armature for a three-dimensional figure can be made by twisting fabric or yarn-covered wires together.

An armature for an animal form

Before attempting this, study the structure of both animals and people, noticing the similarities and differences in the skeleton and the way it is covered. Think of the trunk as a bag, carefully packed with delicate organs and surrounded by a tough cage of bones. This and the arms and legs are all held to a central column of flexible bones which ends in the head. This form is padded to a greater or lesser extent with fat and held in place with a covering of skin.

Think of the wire as the bones, the wadding as fat, the fabric as skin. Look at drawings and models of animals and humans, noting how the bones hang together, the proportion of one limb to another, how each limb bends, and the relationship in size, length and width between one and another. Try to analyse forms and to simplify them.

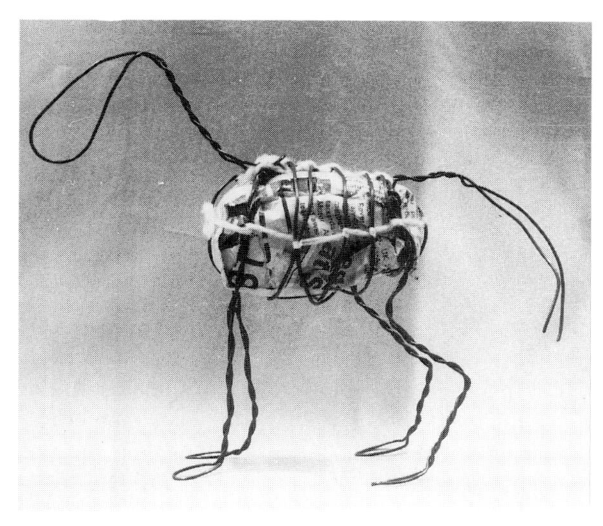

131 A basic animal shape made from wire and newspaper.

Making a form

Make a very simple animal form with wire and newspaper. There are many ways of doing this, of which the following method is only one.

1 Make each pair of legs or arms with one piece of wire. Take a piece of wire which is twice as long as the length of both front legs right up to the backbone. Fold both ends to the middle and twist the wires together.

2 Make a ball of newspaper in the shape of the body. This is rather ovoid with the thick end at the front. Secure with sticky tape.

3 Attach each set of legs to the body. Take a length of wire round the body from front to back, securing with a twist and holding the legs in position, then wrap the wire round and round the body to make a rib cage.

4 Make the head, backbone and tail in one piece with a double wire woven in and out of the wire wrapped round the body.

5 Sew round and round the backbone with a needle and wool or thick cotton to hold everything in position.

6 Sew round the sides in the same way.

It is easier to build the form of a person with the legs, backbone and head made of a double piece of wire, and the body and arms added and secured as above.

At all times it is important to study at first hand the form you are trying to make, at the same time making notes on other forms, not only of animals and humans, but of fish, birds and plants and even buildings and vehicles, to try and see how they are constructed.

Covering wire shapes

Forms can be covered in a number of ways:

- A form made entirely of yarn covered wires will need no further covering.
- A form might be covered with strips of fabric dipped in paste, like papier-mâché.
- Wadding might be wrapped round the form to give more substance, then the whole covered with fabric in the form of clothes to give a much more naturalistic look.

The finished form should be an expression of the individual who has made it, and not a copy of someone else's work.

132 Old man shopping. Wire base padded with newspaper.

Part Three

MATERIALS, TOOLS AND TECHNIQUES

14

Collection and organization of materials

MATERIALS FOR DESIGNING

Ideas and suggestions for design are linked with various techniques throughout the book, so it is very useful to have a collection of graphic materials with which to set about initial designing and planning. This collection need not be large, but it is helpful to have at least a few of the items listed in each section below.

It is important always to start with a good design or plan of campaign for each piece of work, however small. The finished piece will only be as good as the initial design, so it is essential to spend time on this, and get it as near as you can to what you have in mind.

Colours A small box of paints – watercolours, gouache or poster paints, depending on personal taste – is useful, not just for colouring and painting, but also for making prints on paper.

Crayons and pencils are very useful, and these range from watercolours to pastels and oil pastels. These can all be mixed with water or paint to give interesting results. Use what you enjoy most, but try out a new medium now and again. Students' colours are cheaper than artists' colours, but all reliable colours are quite expensive. Cheaper colours can be rather harsh and fade quickly, but are better than nothing.

Wax Wax crayons or cobbler's wax can be used for rubbings, and candlewax for resist.

Markers Pencils and charcoal pencils both range from hard to soft, so start with one of each. Inks make interesting patterns, and can also be mixed with water or paints.

Papers Drawing paper is available in all sizes, colours and weights, either loose or contained in sketchbooks. It can be used for drawing, painting and printing and for cutting or tearing. Browse round a good art shop and look at the paper, then buy a small amount of what appeals to you. It is important that you like what you are using, rather than using it because you think you ought to.

Tissue paper is also sold in a large range of colours. It is interesting to use because of its translucent qualities, and one colour put over another gives a third. It can also be cut, torn and crunched up and glued to give different three-dimensional effects.

Tracing paper is essential for tracing off diagrams, etc.

Glues A glue stick is useful for sticking paper. PVA is an all-purpose glue which can be used to stick paper and fabrics. It can be diluted with water to stiffen fabric or paper shapes. Rubber-based glues can be used where a water-based glue might spoil an already stiffened shape (see Chapter 11).

Drawing implements Pens and brushes, compasses, french curves and a ruler, templates of circles and geometric shapes are all helpful in drawing geometric patterns which need to be repeated and accurate.

A board of some sort is also useful to pin patterns and fabric and to hold things in position. A piece of soft board or cork board is quite sufficient.

RESOURCE MATERIAL

Pictures, cutouts, postcards, photographs, bits of patterned wrapping paper, etc. which are collected as resources can be kept in a looseleaf file or a folder. Write on the back of the picture why you liked it in the first place. Look through the collection every so often for new ideas.

ON THE MOVE

Carry a notebook with you all the time, but particularly to exhibitions and on holiday, just in case you see something interesting. An A5 size cartridge sketchbook is useful because it is a manageable size, or carry a couple of pieces of cartridge paper on a small clipboard. Try to draw fragments and patterns that you see, or if they are surface patterns you might be able to take a rubbing with wax crayon or cobbler's wax. Even a few words will remind you of what you have seen, if you haven't time to draw. Use a pencil case to carry one soft and one hard pencil, and a putty rubber, which is much more successful than an indiarubber.

It is helpful to have some way of recording the colours you see, but it is not always possible to carry round a large box of paints or pencils. Make a 'list' of the colours you use, in paint or crayon, by drawing a column of little boxes, and filling each with one colour. Number each box, and mark the corresponding paint or crayon with the same number. When you see colours you like, use the

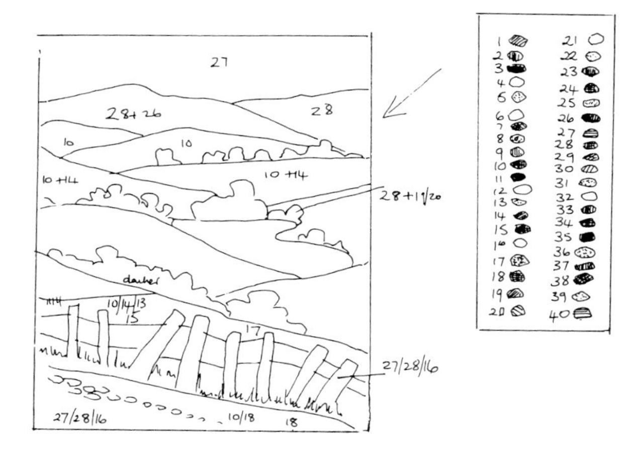

133 How to take notes on colour.

number on your chart to describe them, preferably with any accompanying drawing or diagram. This list of colours can be kept in the back of your notebook.

Two card right angles are useful for isolating areas of pattern but an empty photographic slide holder is just as good and easier to carry. If you keep portable equipment to a minimum you will not be tempted to leave it at home because it is too heavy.

A camera is a good way of recording, but try also to do some drawing, using the photographs as back-up material.

FILING AND STORAGE

Many embroiderers spend time experimenting with a variety of media – drawing, painting, papermaking and modelling – as well as with different techniques in fabric and thread, and the resulting pieces of work need to be stored as reference material in an accessible way. Plastic pockets, more generally used in offices, are available in several sizes and are ideal for storage. Related bits of work, with notes, can be pinned and clipped on paper and put in a plastic pocket, then filed in a looseleaf folder. Make any notes in pencil rather than in ballpoint pen, as it is difficult to remove ink marks from textiles.

COLLECTING AND STORING FABRICS AND THREADS

Fabrics

Quilting is concerned with the manipulation of fabrics. Embroiderers are always interested in fabrics and need no encouragement to collect an enormous quantity and there is a great variety of exciting fabric available not only from shops specializing in furnishings and dressmaking fabrics, but also from market stalls and by mail order. Many embroiderers are turning more and more to plain fabrics which can be dyed and coloured or hand-printed, but there is also a wonderful array of commercially printed fabrics which can be used to good effect. Occasionally these are sold in bundles for patchwork. Groups who are interested in textiles and embroidery often have a sales table at their meetings where small amounts of fabric can be bought.

Storage can be a great problem and many people only have perhaps the space under a bed or on top of a wardrobe to store their materials. Shallow boxes, stacked one on another, are more accessible than deep boxes, and the stacks of shallow wire trays sold as office equipment, or wire trays for kitchen storage, can be used for storing textiles and will make full use of a small space. If you are short of space, you have to be more discriminating about what you keep and it is always a good idea to go through a collection of fabrics regularly, tidy them up and get rid of the ones which are never going to be used.

Medium and large pieces of fabric can be stored rolled on cardboard tubes. Smaller pieces can be ironed and saved in layers in flat boxes. Printed fabrics can be put together, perhaps subdivided into large prints and tiny all-over patterns. Plain fabrics can be kept together. Each type of fabric can also be subdivided into colour groups.

When you buy a fabric, write the fibre content along the selvage, as it is easy to forget and it is often quite important if you want to use it for printing or dyeing.

Wadding, which is extremely bulky, can be wrapped securely in a polythene sack and stored in the loft space or garage.

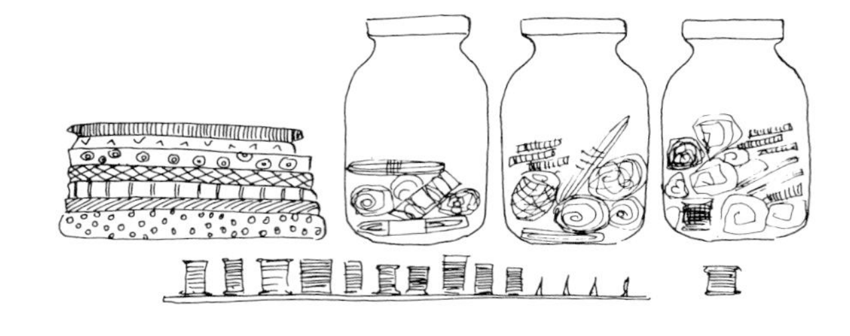

134 Jars and racks of coloured threats and braids can make an attractive display.

Threads

More and more yarns for embroidery and machine embroidery are available every year as more people become interested in textiles as a medium of expression. Like fabrics, threads can easily get out of hand unless they are sorted and stored. Plastic bottles and boxes are very suitable. Threads look inspiring in colour groups. Machine threads can be kept separately in a flat box, where they can easily be picked out and put back. Look out for new and interesting threads which are often advertised in specialist magazines.

HABERDASHERY

Needles

In general, sharp needles are used where the needle passes through rather than between the weave of the fabric – that is, for techniques like quilting and surface embroidery. Tapestry and blunt needles are used for counted thread embroidery like canvas work. For the machine, use a needle which goes with the top fabric unless you are using a very thick or coarse fabric underneath, in which case use a bigger needle. Refer to the chart in the instruction leaflet for the machine.

Long needles for turning rouleaux are now available and are also invaluable for threading yarns through a narrow channel.

135 Needle for making fabric tubes and rouleaux.

Scissors and cutting tools

Scissors must be sharp not only to cut cleanly and accurately, but also to cut through several layers of fabric at once. Have a pair of scissors that are used only for fabric and a separate pair for paper and general use. Take scissors to a reputable person to be sharpened, as a good pair of scissors can be spoilt be bad sharpening.

Craft knives can also be used for cutting fabrics in some circumstances but again, these must be sharp. Keep a craft knife for textiles only.

If you use a stitch ripper to unpick sewing, keep checking that you are not cutting right through to the back (or front) of the work. It is easy to cut away more than you intended.

Pins

Use stainless steel pins at all times. When you are machining several layers of fabric together, the fabrics are placed under great strain, and it is often better to use pins instead of tacking to hold the fabrics in place. The pins should be placed at right angles and not quite touching the projected line of stitching so that the machine can be driven just outside the pin points.

Stiletto

This is a useful tool for making holes, for example in the back layer of a piece of trapunto quilting. Make a hole in woven fabric with a twist, to part the fibres, rather than breaking the threads.

Frames

It is almost always best to use a frame if at all possible. Not only are the materials held flat and taut, but the frame can be rested on the edge of a table leaving both hands free to work. Some frames have table or floor stands.

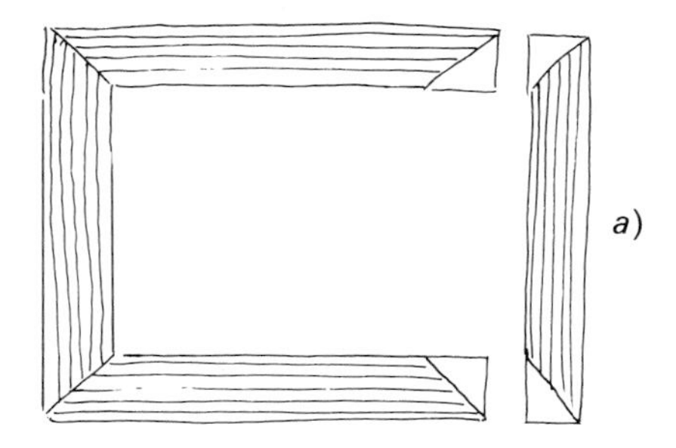

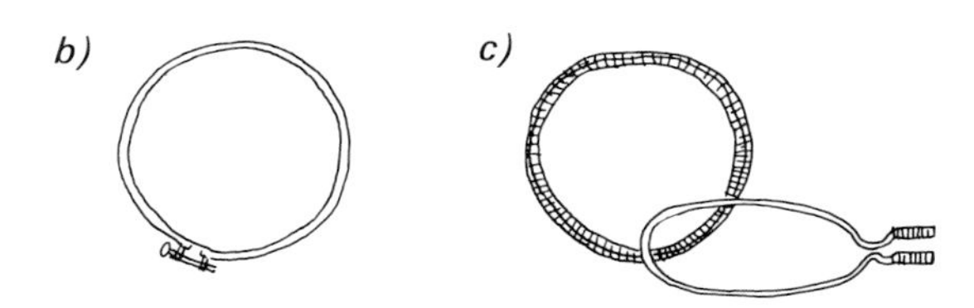

136 Frames for stretching and holding fabric:
(a) Canvas stretchers.
(b) Tambour frame.
(c) Machine embroidery frame.

Canvas stretchers, available from an art shop in a range of sizes, are usually quite suitable for quilting and padding. The background can be attached with drawing pins then the layers of materials will rest on the top.

Slate frames can be used for large pieces of work. The ends of the work are rolled round the end rods of the frame and the sides of the work are stitched to the canvas strips at each side of the frame.

Tambour (round) frames are available in various sizes both in wood and plastic (Fig. 136b). Wood appears to be more successful, as the fabric is held more securely. Bind the inner frame with bias binding.

Frames for machine embroidery have a spring steel inner ring, and are made specially for the sewing machine. They hold the fabric taut and slide easily under the machine foot.

Fabrics in a frame should be taut without being distorted. If the background fabric is held in the frame, the other layers can be tacked on the top. Many of the techniques described in this book use several layers of material. Make sure that any woven fabrics which lie against each other have the weave running in the same direction – otherwise the work will not lie flat. This does not matter if the fabrics are separated by a layer of wadding or a non-woven material like interfacing or plastic.

MARKING FABRICS

●**Marking pens** The recent advent of fabric markers has made drawing designs on fabric much easier as marks can be removed with water. However, always test a small piece of similar fabric first, in case water damages or marks the fabric in some way. Place a rubber band round a marking pen so that it is not confused with an ordinary felt pen.

- A simple pattern can be pinned to the fabric, and short tacking stitches worked round the lines of the design.
- Certain fabrics will show scratchmarks – if so the lines of the design can be scratched with a needle, a small area at a time.

●**Prick and pounce** Although this is time consuming, it gives an accurate copy. Trace the design. Lay the tracing on a padded surface (e.g. an ironing board) and prick along the lines of the design with a needle every 10 cm (4 in.). Turn the paper over and gently smooth it with sandpaper to remove the nibs. Pin the tracing paper to the fabric and gently rub talc (pounce) along the line of holes, or if the fabric is white, mix a small amount of powdered charcoal with the talc. Remove the paper. Join the dots of powder with a very fine brush and watercolour paint. Lines should be almost invisible.

●**Tailor's chalk** This is easy to use, but not very accurate, and is apt to brush off. Sharpen the point of a tailor's chalk pencil for best results.

●**Dressmaker's carbon** This is not recommended, as it is difficult to make a fine line and cannot be removed. It also smudges easily.

In general, the design is marked out on the surface of the top fabric before pinning to other layers of fabric and wadding. If there are only two layers, in trapunto, corded or flat quilting, for example, the design can be marked out on the back of the bottom fabric.

STITCHES

Some stitches and techniques are particularly suitable when they are used in conjunction with rounded and raised surfaces.

137 Needleweaving over a space.

Detached stitches

Detached stitches form a net over the surface of the fabric and are only attached at the edges. There are a number of these, normally used for stumpwork, and they include *detached buttonhole stitch*. *Needleweaving* is worked on warps which can be stretched over any raised surface or hole.

Nets

These can be made by knitting sewing cotton or silk with large needles. Stitches like *raised chain band* and *raised stem stitch* can then be worked over these.

A net can be made on fine, loosely woven fabric like tarlatan by working random *satin stitch* all over. This texture can be cut out and applied. Machine embroidery can be worked on a fabric like organdie which is very closely woven, then cut out and applied. It is not likely to pull out. The cold and hot water dissolvable materials and vanishing muslin that are available for machine embroidery can be used to make an area of texture which might then be sewn to a form.

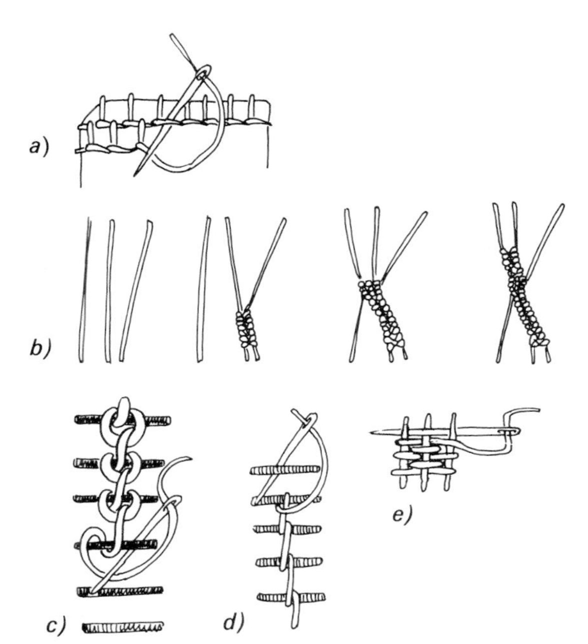

138 Stitches used on three-dimensional forms:
(a) Detached buttonhole.
(b) Needleweaving – pull tight.
(c) Raised chain band – stitches worked round the ladder foundation, and not through the background.
(d) Raised stem stitch.
(e) Weaving.

139 Raised chain band worked on a knitted mesh that has been pulled over a polystyrene meat tray covered with fabric. Knitted fabric is made by knitting fine cotton on large needles.

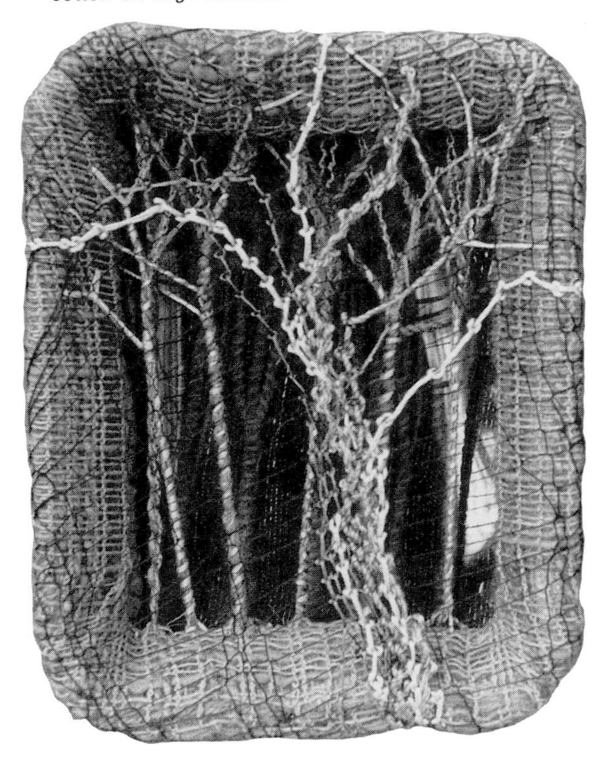

140 The Octopus Garden. Wired, padded leather octopus shape is made in two halves and decorated with cutout leather which is stuck on. The padded hardboard background is decorated with needleweaving and detached buttonhole stitches.

141 Archway. Wadded quilted foliage with stonework made of layers of fabric with some parts cut away. Padded leaf forms are attached to wrapped wire branches. Hand embroidered background.

Suppliers

Many of the ideas in this book are based on using easily obtainable fabrics which are then coloured by hand. *Polyester and synthetic fabrics* for transfer printing, *calico*, *silk*, *organdie*, *felt*, *terylene wadding* and *synthetic stuffing* are all available from branches of John Lewis Partnership.

Canvas stretchers are available from art and craft shops, and most cities and towns have well-stocked shops which are listed in Yellow Pages.

Transparent self-adhesive plastic film is available from stationers and art shops.

More *exotic fabrics, quilting wool,* etc. can be obtained by mail order from:

Barnyarns
Old Pitts Farm
Langrish
Petersfield
Hants
GU32 1RQ

Many more mail order suppliers advertise in craft magazines, including:

Embroidery
PO Box 42B
East Molesey,
Surrey
KT8 9BB

The Quilter
Quilters Guild Magazine
56 Wilcot Road
Pewsey
Wiltshire
SN9 5EC

Crafts
The Crafts Council
8 Waterloo Place
London
SW1 4AT

Educational suppliers such as:

Nottingham Educational Supplies
17 Ludlow Hill Road
Melton Road
West Bridgford
Notts
NG2 6HD

sell fabrics, fabric paints and crayons, frames, etc. and send their catalogue to most schools and educational establishments every year.

Useful addresses

The Embroiderers' Guild
Apartment 41
Hampton Court Palace
East Molesey
Surrey
(The Embroiderers' Guild has branches all over the country which run lectures and workshops on all aspects of embroidery.)

The Quilters' Guild
56 Wilcot Road
Pewsey
Wiltshire
SN9 5EC

The Knitting Craft Group
PO Box 6
Thirsk
N. Yorks
(Produces leaflets on creative knitting and crochet and holds courses for teachers.)

Further reading

Muriel Best, *Stumpwork: Historical and Contemporary Raised Embroidery*, Batsford 1987
Valerie Campbell-Harding, *Flowers and Plants in Embroidery*, Batsford 1986
Averil Colby, *Quilting*, Batsford 1972, 1987
Hannah Frew, *Three-Dimensional Embroidery*, Van Nostrand Reinhold 1975
Edith John, *Needleweaving*, Batsford 1970, 1987
Richard M. Proctor, *The Principles of Pattern for Craftsmen and Designers*, Van Nostrand Reinhold 1969
Guy Scott, *Transfer Printing on Man-Made Fibres*, Batsford 1977
Eirian Short, Quilting: Technique, Design and Application, Batsford 1974
Peter S. Stevens, *Patterns in Nature*, Penguin 1974
Quilting (Search Press Needlecraft Series no. 3)

Index

(Numbers in italics refer to illustrations)